Magento Search Engi Optimization

Maximize sales by optimizing your Magento store
and improving exposure in popular search engines
like Google

Robert Kent

BIRMINGHAM - MUMBAI

Magento Search Engine Optimization

First published: January 2014

Production Reference: 1080114

Published by Packt Publishing Ltd.
Livery Place
35 Livery Street
Birmingham B3 2PB, UK.

ISBN 978-1-78328-857-1

www.packtpub.com

Cover Image by Zarko Piljak (zpiljak@gmail.com)

Credits

Author
Robert Kent

Reviewers
Alejandro Garcia De Frenza
James B. Phillips
Brady Sewall

Acquisition Editors
James Jones
Neha Nagwekar

Commissioning Editor
Shaon Basu

Technical Editors
Neha Mankare
Shiny Poojary
Siddhi Rane

Copy Editors
Sarang Chari
Brandt D'Mello
Adithi Shetty

Project Coordinator
Jomin Varghese

Proofreader
Paul Hindle

Indexers
Monica Ajmera
Mehreen Deshmukh

Production Coordinator
Conidon Miranda

Cover Work
Conidon Miranda

About the Author

Robert Kent is a Magento Certified Developer with over four years of experience using the Magento framework. He currently works at Creare Communications Ltd., one of the UK's largest SEO and web design companies based in the Midlands.

With over 5 years of experience working on a variety of projects across multiple open source frameworks, he has gained expertise in PHP, XML, jQuery, and a wide range of other web-based languages.

Working in an R&D capacity developing extensions, and plugins for both Magento and WordPress, he also plays a key role in developing new techniques and standards for both of these platforms from an SEO perspective.

This is his second book based on Magento, the first book being *Magento Shipping How-To, Packt Publishing*—a guide on how to configure shipping settings within Magento.

I would like to thank James Bavington, Sarah Edwards, and Andrew Allen for all their support, advice, and SEO expertise, all of which were invaluable while writing this book. I'd also like to thank Adam Moss for his share of the development of our Creare SEO extension that will hopefully be ready and waiting (for free) on Magento Connect once this book is published.

About the Reviewers

Alejandro Garcia De Frenza is an Italian/Venezuelan project manager and digital marketing manager possessing a broad mix of technical experience and web marketing and social media skills, with over five years of experience in managing and developing web applications.

He started his career by building websites for clients using technologies such as HTML, CSS, PHP, and MySQL, and then moved on to manage some web development projects before working on some mobile-apps-related projects in Barcelona.

During this period, he developed an interest in the digital marketing field. This curiosity lead him to read many books, experiment, and participate in online training in areas such as SEO, SEM, PPC, Google AdWords and AdSense, Google Analytics, Ad serving technologies, Facebook, and Twitter ads.

He consolidated a great deal of experience in the digital ecosystem while working for General Motors Middle East as a Digital Marketing Manager, and more recently as a Technical Analyst for Google's Doubleclick for publishers in Ireland.

Some of the companies he has worked with are 3M, General Motors, Golden Gekko, and Google. He is always open for collaboration on digital-marketing- and technical-development-related subjects and projects.

James B. Phillips is a freethinking individual who has a true passion for web development and graphic design. Along his career path, he has gained a vast knowledge in online marketing techniques including branding and identity, e-commerce and business web development, **Search Engine Optimization (SEO)**, website performance analysis, cohesive sales and promotion planning, and **Pay Per Click (PPC)** strategy management.

He currently works for the e-commerce division at Honeyville as the lead web developer. Their site can be found at `http://shop.honeyville.com`. He also works under his freelance identity as Legendary Fish. His portfolio can be found at `http://legendary-fish.com`.

Brady Sewall is an e-commerce and online marketing professional with a rich history in graphic design and e-learning development. He has received a degree in multimedia and web design from the Art Institute and has been featured in numerous Magento articles and blogs. He and his father, Gary Sewall, are currently working on various written material about their historical 1929 Gipsy Moth biplane, a favorite pastime for them both.

www.PacktPub.com

Support files, eBooks, discount offers, and more

You might want to visit www.PacktPub.com for support files and downloads related to your book.

Did you know that Packt offers eBook versions of every book published, with PDF and ePub files available? You can upgrade to the eBook version at www.PacktPub.com and as a print book customer, you are entitled to a discount on the eBook copy. Get in touch with us at service@packtpub.com for more details.

At www.PacktPub.com, you can also read a collection of free technical articles, sign up for a range of free newsletters and receive exclusive discounts and offers on Packt books and eBooks.

http://PacktLib.PacktPub.com

Do you need instant solutions to your IT questions? PacktLib is Packt's online digital book library. Here, you can access, read, and search across Packt's entire library of books.

Why Subscribe?

- Fully searchable across every book published by Packt
- Copy and paste, print, and bookmark content
- On demand and accessible via web browser

Free Access for Packt account holders

If you have an account with Packt at www.PacktPub.com, you can use this to access PacktLib today and view nine entirely free books. Simply use your login credentials for immediate access.

Table of Contents

Preface

Optimizing a Magento website can be rather tricky at times, especially when we try to figure out how best to optimize a specific phrase on a particular page while we navigate over 15,000 files and hundreds of different configuration settings.

It can sometimes seem a little daunting, but thankfully, it's not all that bad.

Magento has been built by people who have as much passion about your website as they do about their own software, and as such, they are always looking to improve the internal optimization of their platform.

They've already provided us with a variety of tools that we can use to better prepare our Magento store for search engines. Not only this, but due to the open source nature of the Magento platform, there exists a growing community of developers and SEO specialists who constantly innovate and experiment with different ways to improve the framework.

Like any good e-commerce content management system, Magento allows us to adjust certain elements of each product, category, and CMS page features such as titles, meta information, and headings. Magento is rather good at delivering these simple SEO requirements.

It has, however, its SEO shortcomings, and this book will teach you how to tackle some of the most common issues that may arise.

I hope that with this book, you'll be able to make use of all the tools Magento has provided for you as well as implement some of the more advanced SEO techniques. You should also be able to repair several of those unfortunate SEO flaws that are, to be fair, inherent within almost all large open source frameworks.

The primary goal of optimizing our Magento website—and one that we must always keep at the forefront of our minds—is to enhance the experience for both our customers and search engines.

A better experience for both will give us the best possible chance of increasing our number of visitors, converting those visitors into customers, and boosting the overall sales figures for our Magento website.

What this book covers

Chapter 1, *Preparing and Configuring Your Magento Website*, covers the basic concepts of keyword placement, the roles of the different types of pages, XML sitemap creation, and integrating Google Analytics e-commerce tracking. It also covers the category structure and the default configuration aspects, such as setting up canonical elements, default meta information, and URL structure.

Chapter 2, *Product and Category Page Optimization*, focuses on optimizing our product and category pages and implementing the best practices for elements such as headings, titles, meta information, URL keys, and body content. Page layout, schema integration, and social sharing will also be covered.

Chapter 3, *Managing Internationalization and Multiple Languages*, looks at the best practices for domain structure, store-specific configuration and translation, as well as methods to avoid duplicate content across our multinational store views.

Chapter 4, *Template/Design Adjustments for SEO and CRO*, will cover template manipulation in order to better deliver a clear, organized heading structure as well as how to optimize pagination, product reviews, and the entire checkout experience. It will also cover implementing website-specific microdata, such as breadcrumb and organization schema.

Chapter 5, *Speeding Up Your Magento Website*, will look into why speed is such an important factor for both usability and SEO. It will lead on to show you how it's possible to improve the performance through Magento configuration, server compression, and advanced caching techniques, such as Varnish, for scalability.

Chapter 6, *Analyzing and Tracking Your Visitors*, provides an overview of the features available with Google Analytics to track e-commerce conversions. It also covers ways to better interpret our results using filters, advanced segments, and multi-channel funnels.

Chapter 7, *Technical Rewrites for Search Engines*, shows the various methods available to you in order to fix many URL-related problems that occur within the Magento framework using 301 redirects, URL rewrites, and blocking access to search engines for certain areas using the robots.txt file.

Chapter 8, *Purpose-built Magento Extensions for SEO/CRO*, looks at some of the best SEO- and CRO-related extensions that are available for free and for a price.

What you need for this book

Administrator-level access to a Magento installation is required as well as FTP access in order to edit certain files. This book uses Magento Community Edition 1.8.0.0 as a reference, but most of the content is also applicable to older versions of both the Community and Enterprise editions. It is also recommended that a valid Google account be set up in order to correctly configure both Google Analytics and Google Webmaster Tools..

Who this book is for

This book is highly suited to both Magento developers with an understanding of SEO and on-page SEO specialists who wish to learn more about the possibilities (and limitations) that exist within the Magento platform.

Conventions

In this book, you will find a number of styles of text that distinguish between different kinds of information. Here are some examples of these styles, and an explanation of their meaning.

A block of code is set as follows:

```
<title>Open Source Ecommerce Software &amp; Solutions |
  Magento</title>
<meta name="description" content="Download the Magento Community
  Edition, our free open source ecommerce software solution for
  expert developers and enthusiasts!" />
```

When we wish to draw your attention to a particular part of a code block, the relevant lines or items are set in bold:

```
<urlset xmlns="http://www.sitemaps.org/schemas/sitemap/0.9"
xmlns:xhtml="http://www.w3.org/1999/xhtml">
<url>
<loc>http://store.apple.com/us/browse/home/shop_mac</loc>
<xhtml:link rel="alternate" hreflang="en-us" href="http://store.apple.
com/us/browse/home/shop_mac" />
<xhtml:link rel="alternate" hreflang="en-ae" href="http://store.apple.
com/ae/browse/home/shop_mac" />
<!-- another 40 combinations for this url not shown -->
```

New terms and **important words** are shown in bold. Words that you see on the screen, in menus or dialog boxes for example, appear in the text like this: "Navigate to **Catalog | Manage Categories**".

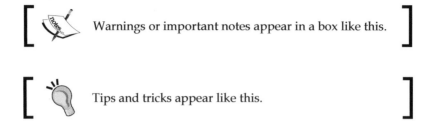

> Warnings or important notes appear in a box like this.

> Tips and tricks appear like this.

Reader feedback

Feedback from our readers is always welcome. Let us know what you think about this book—what you liked or may have disliked. Reader feedback is important for us to develop titles that you really get the most out of.

To send us general feedback, simply send an e-mail to feedback@packtpub.com, and mention the book title through the subject of your message.

If there is a topic that you have expertise in and you are interested in either writing or contributing to a book, see our author guide on www.packtpub.com/authors.

Customer support

Now that you are the proud owner of a Packt book, we have a number of things to help you to get the most from your purchase.

Downloading the example code

You can download the example code files for all Packt books you have purchased from your account at http://www.packtpub.com. If you purchased this book elsewhere, you can visit http://www.packtpub.com/support and register to have the files e-mailed directly to you.

Errata

Although we have taken every care to ensure the accuracy of our content, mistakes do happen. If you find a mistake in one of our books—maybe a mistake in the text or the code—we would be grateful if you would report this to us. By doing so, you can save other readers from frustration and help us improve subsequent versions of this book. If you find any errata, please report them by visiting http://www.packtpub. com/support, selecting your book, clicking on the **errata submission form** link, and entering the details of your errata. Once your errata are verified, your submission will be accepted and the errata will be uploaded to our website, or added to any list of existing errata, under the Errata section of that title.

Piracy

Piracy of copyright material on the Internet is an ongoing problem across all media. At Packt, we take the protection of our copyright and licenses very seriously. If you come across any illegal copies of our works, in any form, on the Internet, please provide us with the location address or website name immediately so that we can pursue a remedy.

Please contact us at copyright@packtpub.com with a link to the suspected pirated material.

We appreciate your help in protecting our authors, and our ability to bring you valuable content.

Questions

You can contact us at questions@packtpub.com if you are having a problem with any aspect of the book, and we will do our best to address it.

1
Preparing and Configuring Your Magento Website

One of the main reasons Magento is fast becoming the e-commerce platform of choice is the fact that, from the ground-up, it has been built with the foreknowledge and flexibility required to optimize every page, every product, and every snippet of code within its framework for search engines. That is assuming you know where to look and how to do it.

There are many similarities between Magento Community Edition and Magento Enterprise Edition, but also a few major differences. Wherever possible, I will try to highlight some of the features that may appear in one or the other of these platforms, and also reference in which version certain features were added or removed.

For the purpose of this guide, we will be using Magento Community Edition 1.8.0.0. As of the time of this writing, it is the latest stable release of the free edition. This should allow store owners, Magento developers, and SEO experts and novices alike access to all of the features contained within this book.

In this chapter, we will cover the following:

- Understanding the structure of a website, the purpose of optimizing for e-commerce, and the relationship between keywords and their position on a website
- Understanding the buying intent of our visitors and how this intent may differ depending on the type of page by which they enter our website
- The roles of **content management system (CMS)** pages and their uses in **search engine optimization (SEO)**
- The importance of the `content`, `title`, and `meta` tags and Magento's default `<head>` data

- How to change your category structure to benefit your SEO campaign
- How to set up an XML sitemap and Google Analytics E-commerce tracking

Focusing on your keywords

An entire book could be written on keyword distribution for e-commerce websites; however, as the aim of this book is to cover the main aspects of optimizing a Magento store, we cannot go into too much depth. Instead, we'll focus on three major considerations when choosing where to place our keywords within a Magento store:

- **Purpose**: What is the purpose of optimizing this keyword?
- **Relevance**: Is the keyword relevant to the page we have chosen to optimize it for?
- **Structure**: Does the structure of the website re-enforce the nature of our keyword?

The purpose for choosing keywords to optimize on our Magento store must always be to increase our sales. It is true that (generically speaking) optimizing keywords means driving visitors to our website, but in the case of an e-commerce website, the end goal—the true justification of any SEO campaign—must be increasing the number of sales. We must then make sure that our visitors not just visit our website, but visit with the intention of buying something.

The keywords we have chosen to optimize must be relevant to the page we are optimizing them on. The page, therefore, must contain elements specifically related to our keyword, and any unrelated material must be kept to a minimum. Driving potential customers to a page where their search term is unrelated to the content not only frustrates the visitor, but also lessens their desire to purchase from our website.

The structure of our website must complement our chosen keyword. Competitive phrases, usually broader phrases with the highest search volume, are naturally the hardest to optimize. These types of keywords require a strong page to effectively optimize them. In most cases, the strength of a page is related to its level or tier within the URL.

For example, the home page is normally seen as being the strongest page suitable for high search volume **broad phrases** followed by a tiered structure of categories, subcategories, and finally, product pages, as this diagram illustrates:

Page:	**top-tier**	**/ second-tier**	/ third-tier.html
Keyword:	**broad phrases**	/ less broad phrases	/ specific phrases

With that said, we must be mindful of all three considerations when matching our keywords to our pages. As the following diagram shows, the relationship between these three elements is vital for ensuring not only that our keyword resides on a page with enough strength to enable it to perform, but also that it has enough relevance to retain our user intent at the same time as adhering to our overall purpose:

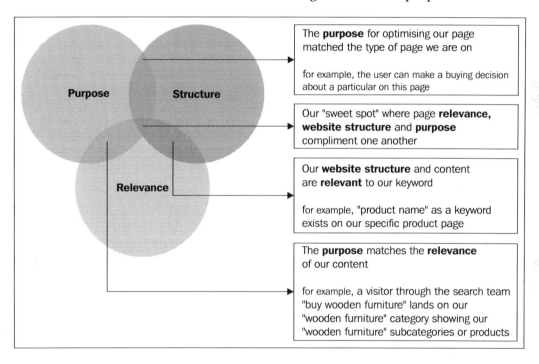

The **purpose** for optimising our page matched the type of page we are on

for example, the user can make a buying decision about a particular on this page

Our "sweet spot" where page **relevance, website structure** and **purpose** compliment one another

Our **website structure** and content are **relevant** to our keyword

for example, "product name" as a keyword exists on our specific product page

The **purpose** matches the **relevance** of our content

for example, a visitor through the search team "buy wooden furniture" lands on our "wooden furniture" category showing our "wooden furniture" subcategories or products

The role of the home page

You may be forgiven for thinking that optimizing our most competitive keyword on the home page would lead to the best results. However, when we take into account the relevance of our home page, does it really match our keyword? The answer is usually that it doesn't.

In most cases, the home page should be used exclusively as a platform for building our **brand identity**. Our brand identity is the face of our business and is how customers will remember us long after they've purchased our goods and exited our website.

> In rare cases, we could optimize keywords on our home page that directly match our brand; for example, if our company name is "Wooden Furniture Co.", it might be acceptable to optimize for "Wooden Furniture" on our home page. It would also be acceptable if we were selling a single item on a single-page e-commerce website.

In a typical Magento store, we would hope to see the following keyword distribution pattern:

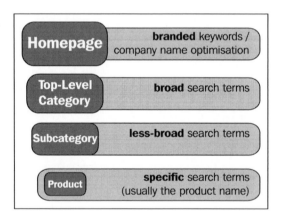

The buying intention of our visitors will almost certainly differ between each of these types of pages. Typically, a user entering our website via a broad phrase will have less of an intention to buy our products than a visitor entering our website through a more specific, product-related search term.

Structuring our categories for better optimization

Normally, our most competitive keywords will be classified as **broad** keywords, meaning that their relevance could be attributed to a variety of similar terms. This is why it makes sense to use top-level or parent categories as a basis for our broad phrases.

To use our example, Wooden Furniture would be an ideal top-level category to contain subcategories such as 'Wooden Tables', 'Wooden Chairs', and 'Wooden Wardrobes', with content on our top-level category page to highlight these subcategories. On the Magento administration panel, go to **Catalog | Manage Categories**. Here, we can arrange our category structure to match our keyword relevance and broadness.

In an ideal world, we would plan out our category structure before implementing it; sadly, that is not always the case. If we need to change our category structure to better match our SEO strategy, Magento provides a simple way to alter our category hierarchy.

For example, say we currently have a top-level category called **Furniture**, and within this category, we have **Wooden Furniture**, and we decide that we're only optimizing for **Wooden Furniture**; we can use Magento's drag-and-drop functionality to move **Wooden Furniture** to become a top-level category.

To do this, we would have to perform the following steps:

1. Navigate to **Catalog | Manage Categories**.
2. Drag our **Wooden Furniture** category to the same level as **Furniture**.

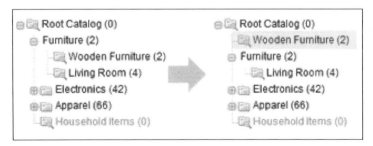

We will see that our URL has now changed from `http://www.mydomain.com/furniture/wooden-furniture.html` to `http://www.mydomain.com/wooden-furniture.html`.

We will also notice that our old URL now redirects to our new URL; this is due to Magento's inbuilt URL Rewrite System. When moving our categories within the hierarchy, Magento will remember the old URL path that was specified and automatically create a redirect to the new location.

This is fantastic for our SEO strategy as 301 redirects are vital for passing on authority from the old page to the new.

A 301 redirect is one of the most useful tools in maintaining a search engine's understanding of our website pages. More information on their importance and how to set up 301 redirects is provided in *Chapter 7, Technical Rewrites for Search Engines*.

If we wanted to have a look at these rewrites ourselves, we could perform the following steps:

1. Navigate to **Catalog | URL Rewrite Management**.
2. From the table, we could find our old request path and see the new target path that has been assigned.

Not only does Magento keep track of our last URL, but any previous URLs also become rewritten. It is therefore not surprising that a large Magento store with numerous products and categories could have thousands upon thousands of rows within this table, especially when each URL is rewritten on a per-store basis.

There are many configuration options within Magento that allow us to decide how and what Magento rewrites for us automatically, and these will be covered within *Chapter 7, Technical Rewrites for Search Engines*.

Another important point to note is that your category URL key may change depending on whether an existing category with the same URL key at the same level had existed previously in the system. If this situation occurs, an automatic incremental integer is appended to the URL key, for example, `wooden-furniture-2.html`.

Magento Enterprise Edition has been enhanced to only allow unique URL keys. To know more, go to `goo.gl/CKprNB`.

Optimizing our CMS pages

CMS pages within Magento are primarily used as information pages. Terms and conditions, privacy policy, and returns policy are all examples of CMS pages that are created and configured within the Magento administration panel under **CMS | Pages**.

By default, the home page of a Magento store is a CMS page with the title **Home Page**. The page that is served as the home page can be configured within the Magento Configuration under **System | Configuration | Web | Default Pages**.

The most important part of a CMS page setup is that its URL key is always relative to the website's base URL. This means that when creating CMS pages, you can manually choose how deep you wish the page to exist on the site. This gives us the ability to create as many nested CMS pages as we like.

Another important point to note is that, by default, CMS pages have no file extension (URL suffix) as opposed to the category and product URLs where we can specify which extension to use (if any).

For CMS pages, the default optimization methods that are available to us are found within the **Page Information** tabs after selecting a CMS page:

- Under the **Page Information** subtab, we can choose our **Page Title** and **URL key**
- Under the **Content** subtab, we can enter our **Content Heading** (by default, this gets inserted into an `<h1>` tag) and enter our body content
- Under the **Meta Data** subtab, we can specify our keywords and description

As mentioned previously, we would focus optimization on these pages purely for the intent of our users. If we were not using custom blocks or other methods to display product information, we would not optimize these information pages for keywords relating to purchasing a product.

Optimizing our titles, content, and meta information

Within CMS, category, and product pages, there will always be the option to specify **Page Title**, **Meta Description**, and **Meta Keywords**, and most importantly, the ability to add content to the page.

If we take a look at a normal **Search Engine Results Page (SERP)** — in this case Google — obtained using the search query `Magento open source download`, we will see that two of these elements are used directly in the result listings (**Title** and **Meta Description**):

> **Open Source** Ecommerce Software & Solutions | **Magento**
> www.**magento**commerce.com/**download** ▾
> **Download** the **Magento** Community Edition, our free **open source** ecommerce software solution for expert developers and enthusiasts!

The code used to display the preceding result is as follows:

```
<title>Open Source Ecommerce Software &amp; Solutions |
    Magento</title>
<meta name="description" content="Download the Magento Community
    Edition, our free open source ecommerce software solution for
    expert developers and enthusiasts!" />
```

Downloading the example code

You can download the example code files for all Packt books you have purchased from your account at `http://www.packtpub.com`. If you purchased this book elsewhere, you can visit `http://www. packtpub.com/support` and register to have the files e-mailed directly to you.

Depending on the search query used, Google may return the meta description, or alternatively, extract a snippet of text from the content that it believes to best represent that page for the given query. The same applies to `title` tags; when a more specific query is used, the default title tag may be changed to better suit the query.

For instance, if we perform a search for `magento download` on Google, instead of the preceding search, we will receive the same page and the same meta description, but a more targeted `title` tag — try it!

An example of Google returning extracted content rather than the meta description can be seen here (through the search phrase `Magento ottoman`):

> **Ottoman - Magento** Commerce Demo Store
> demo.**magento**commerce.com/**ottoman**.html ▾
> The **Magento ottoman** will impress with its style while it delivers on quality. This piece of living room **furniture** is built to last with durable solid wood framing, ...

The meta description that is present on the page is:

```
<meta name="description" content="Ottoman" />
```

From this, we can see that Google has chosen to return the extracted snippet from the product description, most likely due to the meta description being entirely inadequate for the search term.

The best practices for these elements are well documented in SEO circles, and the following is a brief breakdown of each:

- **Title**: The `title` tag should be kept (ideally) to a maximum of 70 to 75 characters. Any title tag longer than this will be truncated in the SERPs to only those first 70 to 75 characters. If we are trying to engage a human being's interest, we need to be able to do that within those first 70 to 75 characters.

- **Meta Description**: The same rules apply to the **Meta Description** field; Google usually only shows approximately 150-160 characters of meta information below the `title` tag in the SERPs. A description longer than this may be truncated and the surplus will not be presented to the user.

- **Meta Keywords**: It has long been acknowledged that most major search engines choose to ignore the meta keyword tag completely, mainly due to keyword stuffing, which was a common practice in past years. Usually, it is more beneficial to remove this tag altogether than to spend time tailoring keywords for individual pages (please see *Chapter 8, Purpose-built Magento Extensions for SEO/CRO*, for ways in which we can remove this tag).

- **Content**: This is a contentious subject; however, the accepted guidelines are that 400+ words of unique, quality, and relevant content per page should stand you in good stead with all the major search engines. There are also reports of 2000+ words of quality content providing the best results and resulting in the best rankings. At this time, it is unknown if there is an upper-limit to the amount of content deemed acceptable on any given page. The truth is that it becomes harder to write relevant, quality content the longer that content becomes.

For more information, please visit:

- Content Length (`quicksprout.com`): `goo.gl/WNopcC`
- Title Tags (`moz.com`): `goo.gl/LM9efj`
- Meta Descriptions (`moz.com`): `goo.gl/fpgSTi`
- Meta Keywords (`google.com`): `goo.gl/CJg89b`

Adjusting our Magento configuration for SEO

A really quick and easy adjustment we can make to our entire website URL structure is to remove the default `index.php` string that is appended to the base URL—for example, `http://www.mydomain.com/index.php/my-product.html`—and also auto-redirect to our base URL if the non-www version of our domain is entered.

In order to achieve these small fixes, we should perform the following steps:

1. Navigate to **System | Configuration | Web | Search Engines Optimization** and set **Use Web Server Rewrites** to **Yes** to remove `index.php`.

2. Within this same section but under **URL Options**, set **Auto-redirect to Base URL** to **Yes (301 Moved Permanently)**.

As long as our server has been configured correctly and our default `.htaccess` file is in place, Magento will automatically remove the `index.php` string from our URLs and continue to serve our pages as normal. By performing the preceding steps we will also be setting up an automatic SEO-friendly redirect for non-www versions of our URLs.

> Unfortunately, by default, all pages will now be accessible with and without URLs containing `index.php`. In order to resolve this, we can use canonical tags—canonical tags do not contain `index.php` within the URL once this change has been made.

As mentioned previously, Magento comes equipped with the ability to rewrite URLs for category and product pages. Depending on the configuration we have decided upon, Magento will create entries within its `core_url_rewrite` table in the database to accommodate changes to the URL key of a category, a product, or the categorization of a product within our store.

In order to adjust how Magento rewrites our URLs, we can change certain options within **System | Configuration | Catalog | Search Engine Optimizations** as shown in the following screenshot:

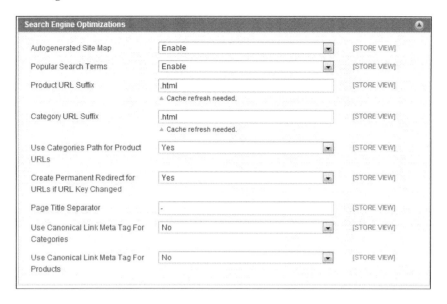

If we take a quick look at this section, we will notice that there are many options, all of which require explanation:

- **Autogenerated Site Map**: If enabled, this creates two pages on our Magento website that display links to our categories and products: `www.mydomain.com/catalog/seo_sitemap/category/` and `www.mydomain.com/catalog/seo_sitemap/product/`, respectively.

- **Popular Search Terms**: This enables a page that displays your most popular search terms. This is not hugely relevant for SEO and should only be used as a tool aimed at your visitors rather than for search engines.

- **Product URL Suffix**: This adds data to the end of the URL for product pages; the default is `.html`.

- **Category URL Suffix**: This is the same as the preceding item but is meant for category pages.

- **Use Categories Path for Product URLs**: With this enabled, Magento will include the category URL key within the URL structure for our product pages (for example, www.mymagento.com/category-url/product.html). When used in conjunction with **Use Canonical Link Meta Tag for Products**, this setting may impact our link building capabilities for our cached product pages.

> External links built for our category-level product URLs are not automatically 301 redirected to our new canonical product URL. This can be remedied by following the *Creare SEO by CreareGroup* section in *Chapter 8, Purpose-built Magento Extensions for SEO/CRO*.

- **Create Permanent Redirect for URLs if URL Key Changed**: This setting will automatically create a rewrite if we ever change the URL key attribute for a CMS, category, or product page.

- **Page Title Separator**: This is a character that separates the specified page title when browsing through categories and subcategories.

- **Use Canonical Link Meta Tag for Categories**: With this setting enabled, all categories will contain a new tag within their HTML instructing search engines where the primary version of the current category page can be found.

- **Use Canonical Link Meta Tag for Products**: This is the same as the preceding item but will instruct the search engine to look for a primary version of any given product page.

Duplicate content is the main worry when it comes to e-commerce websites. The ability to double-categorize products is both a blessing and a curse; a blessing for users who may look for a certain product under two separate categories, but a curse for search engines, which will find identical content on two separate URLs.

> It is important to note that research suggests major search engines such as Google and Bing can detect when a website is classified as an e-commerce site and can make allowances for duplicate product pages.
>
> However, it is always a good practice to ensure that, whenever possible, all steps have been taken to make this task of deducing the primary page as easy as possible for search engines.

The canonical HTML tag has been given to us for this specific purpose. It is used to point search engines to a specific URL—the URL that we want our search engine to display in the SERPs.

Here is an example of a canonical tag:

```
<link rel="canonical" href="http://www.mydomain.com/ottoman.html" />
```

For categories, the canonical tag is used to determine the static URL of that category. That is to say that when filters or pagination features are activated, the parameters appended to the URL should not be cached as separate duplicates of our category page.

In order to set up our Magento store for best optimization practice, we would want to set our configuration as follows:

1. Navigate to **System | Configuration | Catalog | Search Engine Optimizations**.
2. Set **Use Categories Path for Product URLs** to **No**.
3. Set **Use Canonical Link Meta Tag for Categories** and **Use Canonical Link Meta Tag for Products** to **Yes** and then click on **Save Config**.
4. Navigate to **System | Index Management** next to **Catalog URL Rewrites** and click on **Reindex Data**.

When we set **Use Categories Path for Product URLs** to **No**, we were telling Magento to serve our canonical product link to our users when they browse our categories. We could have set this to **No** even if we hadn't enabled our canonical tag for products; however, product URLs will always exist in the same two places. For example:

- `http://www.mydomain.com/furniture/living-room/ottoman.html`
- `http://www.mydomain.com/ottoman.html`

Ideally, we want to restrict both our users and search engines to only one version of our product page.

Restricting our users to the single URLs (without categories) will allow us to maintain consistent link-building equity for each page. Directing search engines via the canonical tag will help resolve duplicate listings in the SERPs and any algorithmic penalties attributed to duplicate content violations.

Default <head> settings

As Magento is such a large system, every element cannot be expected to be manually entered before being used in the system. That is why Magento has a fall-back process in place for a lot of configurable options. These can be found within **System | Configuration | Design | HTML Head**.

For SEO purposes, the main default elements we are interested in are:

- **Default Title**
- **Default Description**
- **Default Keywords**
- **Default Robots**

These defaults are intended to display content to both users and search engines wherever we have failed to populate the relevant field in our administration panel—primarily for CMS pages and categories.

In many instances, **Default Title** will only be used when a custom development has been made and a title is not specified within the Layout XML, the PHP controller file, or some form of admin configuration. **Default Description**, however, will be used whenever **Meta Description** is left unpopulated on a category or CMS page.

Duplicate meta description and title tags are extremely bad for usability. For any page that we wish to perform well in search engines, we must ensure that we have a unique meta description, and if possible, a unique title. This allows search engines to better discern individual pages and also makes it easier for users who are searching for our content to instantly find the correct page among multiple results.

For products, Magento handles the default meta description and keywords tags differently; they are usually prepopulated with the following information:

- **Meta Title**: If this is left unpopulated, the product name will be used
- **Meta Description**: If this is left unpopulated, the product description will be used
- **Meta Keywords**: If this is left unpopulated, the product name will be used

As our products should all be unique, this inbuilt system is a useful tool for large Magento websites that are set live without all product meta information being initially entered.

As we know, Magento should only serve up these default attributes if we have failed in some way to enter the information ourselves. To maintain a good standard of usability for these types of situations, it is a best practice to populate these fields with relevant data (this data can also be modified on a per-store basis):

- Navigate to **System** | **Configuration** | **Design** | **HTML Head** and populate the following:

    ○ Set **Default Title** to be relevant to our store or company name

- ° Set **Default Description** to contain important information, perhaps even contact information for our website (for example, a telephone number)
- ° Set **Default Keywords** to our company name

An example of this could be:

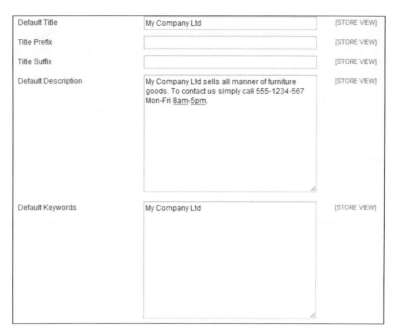

Finally, within our **HTML Head** section is a small but extremely important option called **Default Robots**.

When a Magento website is under development on a test URL, we would normally find the value of this select field to be **NOINDEX, NOFOLLOW**, essentially blocking search engine spiders from accessing any page in the Magento system. It is therefore of paramount importance that, once the website is launched on the live domain, this select option is set to **INDEX, FOLLOW**, or our Magento website may never be indexed by search engines!

A quick reference for each of the available four options is as follows:

- **INDEX, FOLLOW**: Allow my pages to be indexed by the search engine and analyze links found on this page
- **NOINDEX, FOLLOW**: Do not index my pages but go ahead and analyze links found on this page
- **INDEX, NOFOLLOW**: Please index my page but do not harvest any links found on this page
- **NOINDEX, NOFOLLOW**: Please do not index my page and do not harvest any links found on this page

 As well as the `<meta name="robots" />` tag, it is highly encouraged to back up any robot-specific queries with a `robots.txt` file. We will talk more about the `robots.txt` file in *Chapter 7, Technical Rewrites for Search Engines*.

XML sitemap

We all know that search engines can identify pages on a website via its internal (and external) linking structure. However, the most comprehensive and accessible method of providing our website structure to search engines by far is via a valid XML sitemap that is uploaded to a search engine's Webmaster Tools (for example, Google Webmaster Tools).

Naturally, the development team behind Magento realized that manually creating an XML sitemap from all the ever-changing pages, products, and category URLs would be an impossible task. Therefore, they developed their very own XML Sitemap Generator.

In order to generate our XML sitemap, we must first configure its contents. Go to **System | Configuration | Google Sitemap** and configure **Frequency** and **Priority** for our main page types. We can also configure how often we want to generate our sitemap.

Depending on our Magento store, we may decide that our categories are the most important pages. They're our most optimized pages and we want search engines to index them first. Our next most important pages would be our individual product pages; we want those to appear in search engines for customers searching specifically for our product names. The page type with the least priority would normally be our CMS pages.

> As mentioned previously, the home page in Magento is classified as a CMS page; therefore, based on our specifications, it will receive a lower priority. In addition, the home page URL or `<loc>` will be set as `http://www.mydomain.com/home`, which is not how we want our home page to appear.
>
> These are both problems that can be overcome via Magento extensions mentioned in *Chapter 8, Purpose-built Magento Extensions for SEO/CRO*.

The priority is simply a value that is passed to Google in order for it to prioritize the list of pages it will index; it will then (supposedly) do so programmatically.

Based upon our chosen SEO campaign, we would set the priority higher for those pages we are optimizing. Therefore, if we are optimizing our categories and products more than CMS pages (recommended) we would set their priorities to match the following:

1. Within **Categories Options**, set **Frequency** to **Daily** and **Priority** to 1.
2. Within **Products Options**, set **Frequency** to **Daily** and **Priority** to 0.8 (or anything less than 1 and more than we are about to set the CMS pages to).
3. Within **CMS Pages Options**, set **Frequency** to **Weekly** and **Priority** to 0.25.
4. Within **Generation Settings**, set **Enabled** to **Yes**, **Start Time** to **01 00 00** (01:00 a.m.), and **Frequency** to **Daily**, and enter your e-mail address into the **Error Email Recipient** field.
5. Click on **Save Config**.

In the end, we should have something that looks like this:

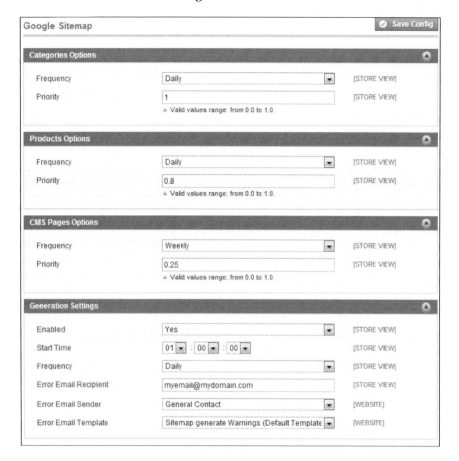

In order for our generation settings to automatically generate our sitemap, the Magento CRON must be enabled. A quick tutorial on how to do this can be found here: goo.gl/q3ngaJ.

Our next step is to make sure that we have an XML sitemap that will be updated based on these settings. To do this, we need to first create one as follows:

1. Navigate to **Catalog | Google Sitemap** and click on **Add Sitemap**.

2. For **Filename**, enter sitemap.xml.

3. For **Path**, we can specify a path, but we would usually place an XML sitemap on the root of our website (enter /).

4. If we have multiple store views, we can enter a specific sitemap for each **Store View** (in which case we would change our filename to suit the convention, for example, `sitemap_en.xml` for English).

5. Click on **Save & Generate**.

This should generate an XML sitemap in our chosen path with our chosen filename. We can test this by visiting our `path/filename` in the URL, for example, `http://www.mydomain.com/sitemap.xml`.

> If an error message appears informing you that the specified directory is not writable, please make sure that the folder specified under **Path** has sufficient privileges to allow the system to write a file—usually 775, or failing that, 777.

Once we have confirmed that our XML sitemap is set up and working correctly, we now need to make sure that it has been submitted to our chosen search engine—Google.

There are two ways to do this, but for safety's sake, we would usually perform both:

1. Open the `robots.txt` file and add in
   `Sitemap: http://www.mydomain.com/sitemap.xml`.

2. Log in to Google Webmaster Tools (`www.google.com/webmasters/tools/`), click on our website (or add our site if we need to create one), and then, within **Crawl**, click on **Sitemaps** and **Add/Test Sitemap**.

Google Analytics

SEO would be obsolete if there wasn't a way to analyze the flow of traffic onto (and through) our optimized website.

There are many analytics packages out there, but the most popular by far is Google Analytics (`http://www.google.com/analytics/`).

In order to set up Analytics effectively on our Magento store, we will need to enter our Google Analytics Account Number (tracking ID) in the administration panel. It is also recommended that we activate e-commerce tracking from within our Google Analytics account.

In order to do this, perform the following steps:

1. Log in to our Google Analytics account and navigate to our particular website's account page.

2. Click on **Admin**.

3. Within this section, we should see three columns: **Account, Property,** and **View**. If we wish to find out our **Tracking ID**, click on **Property Settings** under the **Property** column; we can then copy/paste our **Tracking ID** from here.

4. To turn on **E-commerce tracking**, we should click on **View Settings** within the **View** section and then scroll down to **Ecommerce Settings** and ensure that the toggle is set to **ON**.

5. Now that we have our tracking ID and have enabled **E-commerce tracking** in Google Analytics, we should navigate to our Magento administration panel and then go to **System | Configuration | Google API | Google Analytics**.

6. Paste in our tracking ID into the **Account Number** field, set **Enable** to **Yes**, and then click on **Save Config**.

Now that we have set up analytics, we will find a whole plethora of information is now available to us, including the ability to track revenue by source and to work out our most effective conversion paths. We'll look at more advanced tracking methods in *Chapter 6, Analyzing and Tracking Your Visitors*.

To double-check that our website is calling out the Google Analytics JavaScript code, we can navigate to our home page and then, within the browser, view the page source. Just inside the <body> tag, we should find code similar to the following:

```
<!-- BEGIN GOOGLE ANALYTICS CODEs -->
// our <script> tag containing our tracking code here
<!-- END GOOGLE ANALYTICS CODE -->
```

If we do not see this code, it could be that the template file has been edited and the tag that includes our Google Analytics code has been removed. If this is the case, we should double-check our standard template files (`1column.phtml`, `2columns-left.phtml`, `2columns-right.phtml`, and `3columns.phtml`, usually found within `app/design/frontend/[package]/[theme]/template/page`) to make sure that these two snippets of code are in place:

- `<?php echo $this->getChildHtml('after_body_start') ?>`
- `<?php echo $this->getChildHtml('before_body_end') ?>`

Summary

In this chapter, we learned how to effectively distribute our keywords across our Magento store, how we should optimize our different page types, and the pivotal role keyword relevance has on SEO.

We have also scratched the surface of default optimization techniques such as using `title` tags and `meta` tags and saw how the content of a website can affect search engine rankings. We'll be exploring these in greater detail in later chapters.

We have configured our Magento store to best protect our website against duplicate content issues using the canonical tag, ensuring that our product pages are restricted to a single URL.

Our website is now accessible to search engines and our XML sitemap has been generated and optimized for our content. Google Analytics has also been successfully integrated to better enable us to track and measure how well our website converts visits into sales.

In the next chapter, we will be looking at how to optimize our category and product pages in greater detail.

2
Product and Category Page Optimization

In the previous chapter, we touched upon the importance of category pages for keyword distribution. Generally speaking, category pages are perfect to optimize "broader" search phrases as the names and content of our categories tend to automatically relate with those types of phrases.

For example, if we were optimizing for "Wooden Dining Chairs" and we had a wooden dining chairs category, it would make sense to use it to optimize this keyword rather than create a separate landing page. The category page is the most obvious place for users to look for "Wooden Dining Chairs".

Within this chapter, we will be looking at how to best format category pages for both visitors and search engines. We'll also be looking at optimizing our product pages to bring better conversions through our website and how to improve their appearance in the **SERPs** (**search engine result pages**).

In this chapter, we will be learning how to:

- Edit our title, meta description, and URL key to better optimize product and category pages for SEO and their appearance in the SERPs
- Create and format our content to better suit customers and search engines
- Better sell our products on our product pages
- Implement semantic SEO using schema markup
- Use Twitter, Facebook, and Google widgets to help share our product page

Optimizing titles and descriptions for the SERPs

Adjusting **Page Title** and **Meta Description** are the easiest and most obvious optimization improvements we can make to our category and product pages.

As mentioned previously, the role of the **Page Title** and **Meta Description** fields is to represent our page in the SERPs.

Although **Page Title** certainly plays a role in search engine ranking factors, **Meta Description** is deemed to be of far less value when it comes to ranking websites. What is clear however is that, when displayed in the SERPs, both of these elements play vital roles in advertising our page.

When optimizing our page titles and descriptions, the main questions we should be asking ourselves are:

- Is this relevant to the page?
- Is it descriptive of the content and the search intent of the user?

The common problem when incorporating keywords into page titles and descriptions is that, if we're not careful, it's all too easy to lose relevance.

Firstly, let's consider page titles. The general rules for well-structured page titles are that:

- They must be no greater than 70-75 characters
- They must contain our keywords
- The keywords should appear towards the beginning of the page title (unless it is the home page, where our brand name would appear towards the beginning)
- In all other cases other than the home page, we would generally see our brand name at the end of our page title separated by a dash (-) or pipe (|)

These are general rules of course, but there are many exceptions, and it all depends on the SEO strategy we are implementing for our website.

If we take a look at the top five organic results for the phrase "Wooden Dining Chairs" on Google.com, we will see a variety of page titles and meta description implementations and some interesting results as shown in the following screenshot:

Amazon.com: **Wood - Dining Chairs** / Dining Room Furniture ...
www.amazon.com/s?rh=n%3A3733821%2Cp_n_material... ▾
Results 1 - 24 of 3771 - Online shopping for **Dining Chairs** from a great selection of
Furniture & Decor; Dining Room Furniture & more at everyday low prices.
Beech - Birch - Cedar - Cherry

Wood Dining Chairs | Overstock.com: Buy Dining Room & Bar ...
www.overstock.com › ... › Dining Room & Bar Furniture › Dining Chairs ▾
Wood Dining Chairs: Dining Chairs for everyday discount prices on Overstock.com!
Everyday free shipping over $50*. Find product reviews on Dining Room ...

Light **Wood Dining Chairs** | Wayfair
www.wayfair.com › ... › Kitchen & Dining Chairs ▾
Shop Wayfair for Light **Wood Dining Chairs** to match every style and budget. Enjoy
Free Shipping on most stuff, even big stuff.

Dining Chairs | Wooden, Plastic & Fabric **Dining Chairs** at John Lewis
www.johnlewis.com › Home & Garden ▾
Shop for Dining Chairs at John Lewis. Buy from traditional **wooden dining chairs** to
designer collaborations such as Kartell, Neptune & Vitra. Free delivery on ...

Solid **Wood Dining Chairs** | eBay
www.ebay.co.uk › Home, Furniture & DIY › Furniture ▾
£39.80 - In stock
25+ items - Find great deals on eBay for Solid **Wood Dining Chairs** in ...
6 matching dining room chairs. Collect West Sussex.   2h 50m left.   £14.69.
6 wooden dining chairs.   2h 55m left.   £18.05.

From these results, we can clearly see that these pages are not all using the same title
and description format, but they are obviously still ranking well in the search results.

The obvious patterns we can see when we compare these results to our general rules
are that:

- All results contain the brand name in the page title
- Four out of five contain the brand name in the description
- All results contain at least one combination related to our search term

We can see that the top most results in our list are exceptions to our basic rules, so
we cannot simply contribute their rankings to how their page titles and descriptions
are set out. Most if not all of these websites are well-known brand names; they are
naturally more prominent in the search results due to other important SEO factors,
such as domain authority and the links they have accumulated.

For instance, Amazon.com ranks position one (top of the first page—organically) for this phrase—even though it checks the least number of boxes in our general title and description rules. Although we can't all be lucky enough to be optimizing a website with so much domain authority, what we can take heart from is that four of the other five results are also well-known brands and are mostly following our page title convention.

These results highlight that when analyzing search listings and our competition, it's important to keep in mind that what is shown is not always the best practice. There are numerous factors involved, and those who rank at the top may be making up for lack of best practice in other more important areas.

If we now take a look at the meta description of these results, we can see that not only does each result contain a mention of our keyword (or a keyword that Google deems to be a close/relevant match), but also the context of each description relates to "purchasing" or "buying" these particular items.

Each result features the word "shop", "buy", "prices", "product", or "deal" among many other similar terms related to purchasing. Although not necessarily a ranking factor in itself, the use of these terms prepares the user for the product-related content they will see when visiting these pages.

Due to the fact that search engines such as Google highlight relevant search terms within the results, there has been a common mistake among webmasters to try to fit in as many mentions of the search term as possible—simply to try to stand out from the crowd. This type of "spamming" meta descriptions will almost certainly lead to problems maintaining relevance and purpose.

What we should be aiming towards is a fair balance between mentioning our keyword and the context of that keyword within the description.

My favorite two descriptions from these results and those which I personally would naturally find myself reading and clicking on are:

Light **Wood Dining Chairs** | Wayfair
www.wayfair.com › ... › Kitchen & Dining Chairs ▾
Shop Wayfair for Light **Wood Dining Chairs** to match every style and budget. Enjoy Free Shipping on most stuff, even big stuff.

Dining Chairs | Wooden, Plastic & Fabric **Dining Chairs** at John Lewis
www.johnlewis.com › Home & Garden ▾
Shop for Dining Chairs at John Lewis. Buy from traditional **wooden dining chairs** to designer collaborations such as Kartell, Neptune & Vitra. Free delivery on ...

The search term appears very naturally within these descriptions (it has maintained its relevance), there's important additional information present (for example, free shipping), and the entire message leaves the user in no doubt as to what the content of each of these pages will contain.

Adjusting our category titles and descriptions

In order to implement these general principles into our Magento categories, we would first of all want to set our brand name up as an automatic title suffix.

To do this, within the administration panel:

1. Navigate to **System | Configuration | Design | HTML Head**.
2. Within this section, set **Title Suffix** to "- Brand Name" (using either "-" or " | " as shown in the following screenshot) and click on **Save Config**.

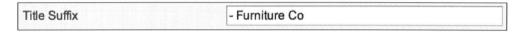

Title Suffix	- Furniture Co

Now that our suffix has been set up, we will not need to manually enter this into every page title. This will be done for us automatically.

We should now see that our Magento category names will be (by default):

[Category Name] [Title Suffix], for example, `Wooden Furniture - Furniture Co`

In many cases this would suffice, as our search term may automatically match our category name; however, if we do need to tweak our category page title, Magento provides us with the ability to change it through the admin interface using the following steps:

1. Navigate to **Catalog | Manage Categories**.
2. Select a category on the left by clicking on the name of our category and then, within the **General Information** tab, enter our new page title. Finally, click on **Save Category**.

Changing **Page Title** within **Manage Categories** is useful if we wish to modify our page title slightly but keep our category name the same—for use within navigation elements and so on.

In order to edit our category meta descriptions, we can do so with the following step:

1. Within the **General Information** tab of our chosen category, set our **Meta Description** field to a 160 character customer-targeted description mentioning our chosen search term.

An example of a targeted category description for "Wooden Dining Chairs" would be:

```
Shop at Furniture Co Ltd for a wide range of wooden dining chairs
available at unbelievable prices. We offer free shipping for any
order over $100.
```

As mentioned in the previous chapter, it is imperative that we make sure we have entered our meta description for all of our categories; otherwise, we may be penalized for duplicate meta description tags.

Unfortunately, unlike the page title, our default fallback for our description will not take into account our category name, but will instead bring back the default description that was set within **System | Configuration | Design | HTML Head**.

Adjusting our product titles and descriptions

All of the examples mentioned in the preceding section have been specific to category pages; however, our product pages are slightly different, and that is once again due to the Magento meta-data fallback process.

A Magento store could have any number of categories and products. Generally, the number of categories on a Magento store is relatively small and, therefore, specifying the page title and meta description for each is relatively easy. However, there can sometimes be hundreds of thousands of products and, therefore (depending on the resources at hand), it is a long and arduous process to write quality, relevant descriptions for each product.

The fallback for products takes this into account, and rather than serving up the default meta description will endeavor using a snippet from our product description used on the page.

The downside of this is that only the first 200 or so characters are taken from our product description, which may or may not be the most relevant of all the text we have written. These 200-220 characters might also contain HTML—which should not be used within a meta description.

 It is advisable that (where possible) simple custom meta descriptions that are hand-written would be more beneficial for display in search engines. The fallback should only be used as a temporary fix until this can be achieved.

Page titles, however, are generally automatically created using our product name and are therefore already optimized for our product-specific keywords. Much like categories, both our page titles and meta descriptions for our products can be edited via the administration panel:

1. Navigate to **Catalog | Manage Products** and select a product.

2. Click on the **Meta Information** tab and enter **Meta Title** (if the page title needs to be slightly different to the product name) and **Meta Description**.

The same rules of relevance and purpose apply when writing our meta descriptions and titles for products. We need to make sure that when viewed in the SERPs, the intention of what our page is about is clear to the user—essentially prequalifying our visitors to those interested in perhaps purchasing our product.

The following screenshot shows a few good examples of product pages within the search results:

TaylorMade R1 Driver at Golfsmith.com
www.golfsmith.com › Golf store › Golf Clubs › Men's Golf Clubs ▾
★★★★☆ Rating: 4.3 - 30 reviews
Buy the **TaylorMade R1 Driver** for less at Golfsmith.com. Shop Golfsmith for the best selection of Drivers.

Canon EOS 500D - EOS Digital SLR Camera - Canon UK
www.canon.co.uk › ... › Product Finder › EOS Digital SLR Camera ▾
The **Canon EOS** 450D New Digital Camera from **Canon** Europe has a 12.2 mega pixel CMOS sensor, offering 3.5fps and a lightweight uncompromising ...

A few key pieces of information to note:

- Product name always comes first
- Brand name is always mentioned in the title and description
- Meta description is either a clear indication of selling the item or can be a detailed description of the key features of the product

 If the brand of our products happens to be our own company's brand name, we would restrict the usage of our brand term to just one instance.

If pricing details are fixed or changes infrequently, it may also be beneficial to include pricing information within the meta description.

Optimizing our URL keys

The other obvious element on a search engine's results page, besides the title and description (and other schema implementations, which we'll move onto in a moment), is the page URL.

The general consensus within the SEO community is that URL keys should be relevant to our destination page, in lowercase, and simple for the user to interpret.

By default, Magento will try to set our URL key as our product or category name followed by our chosen file extension. For SEO purposes, this is perfectly acceptable, and we wouldn't want to change these from their defaults too much.

As covered in the previous chapter, we would simply want to make sure that our URLs are as clean and simple as possible by performing simple tasks such as:

- Removing the `index.php` file from our URLs
- Using our canonical URL for products (`www.mydomain.com/my-product-url.html`)

URLs should be user-friendly wherever possible—this means short and descriptive of the content. A shorter URL is also more likely to be shared via social networks and other websites, mainly due to character limitations.

If our URL keys are too long or contain redundant words that may not be used by search engines for a given search query (such as "and" and "for"), we can edit our URL keys using the following steps:

For products:

1. Navigate to **Catalog | Manage Products** and select a product. Within the **General Information** tab (by default), we can set our **URL Key** field and click on **Save Product**.

For categories:

1. Navigate to **Catalog | Manage Categories** and select a category from the left-hand side menu. Then, within the **General Information** tab, set our **URL Key** field and click on **Save Category**.

Layout and content considerations

When optimizing the content on our pages, we must always make sure that the primary purpose of our content is to engage our visitors—not pander directly to search engines. The more beneficial our page is to our users, the greater the chance that search engines will want to present our page to its own users.

Well-structured category and product pages are essential for any e-commerce website. The ease in which a customer can browse the website and add a product to the cart is fundamental in making sure that our store converts visits into sales.

This is normally dependent on the layout of the website and not only affects our conversion rates, but also visitor bounce rates and time on page, which are both important ranking factors for SEO.

Category page layout

For categories, Magento provides us with the following default tools in which to display content to the user:

- The ability to add a category description, image, and thumbnail
- The ability to display a static block/products or both
- The ability to show products in a grid or list view format, change how they are sorted, and change how many to show per page
- The ability to show layered navigation (product filters)
- The ability to define our own layout (and with this the ability to change any aspect of the page)

As we can see, Magento has provided us with a lot of options to change the way our categories appear to our customers. A skilled frontend developer will be able to create a bespoke design for any category page and move any of the elements around in order to meet the design brief.

We won't go into too much detail about design principles here, but instead we'll focus on the SEO aspects of how a category page is put together, what the best practices are, and how best to configure those settings to better serve our visitors.

If we use our example from before of the top five sites for the phrase "Wooden dining chairs", we will see a general pattern emerge for our layout as shown in the following screenshot:

The general pattern that emerged for our layout is as follows:

- Filters are located on the left-hand side, and this section takes up roughly 25 percent of the screen space. This is so that visitors can find them quickly and easily but at the same time not be distracted too greatly from our most important area — the products.

- The product area is roughly 70-75 percent of the screen space and, with the exception of eBay (on the far right-hand side), is laid out in a grid structure. This leaves the visitor in no doubt as to the primary subject of the page.

- The pagination and sort by attributes are located just above (and below) the product grid—again another accessibility feature, but one that does not detract from the focus of the products.

This setup is deemed to be the best practice (particularly for desktop users) at this moment in time, and we should try to replicate a similar setup in our Magento store.

The general steps to take in order to set our category pages to a similar layout are to make sure that:

1. We are using the two-column template with the left-hand side bar for our category pages. We can either change this by default within our layout XML or, if we want to do it per category, navigate to **Manage Categories | Custom Design | Page Layout** and set it to **2 columns with left bar**.

2. To make sure our category has layered navigation enabled, we can do this by checking that within **Display Settings**, **Is Anchor** is set to **Yes**.

3. We have set grid mode as our default display mode. To do this, we must check that **System | Configuration | Catalog | Frontend | List Mode** is set to **Grid (default) / List** or simply **Grid Only**.

Product page layout

Product pages, as we saw with category pages, tend to maintain a standard layout. If we were to take a look at the product page layout of the first result on each of those previous categories, we would notice the following similarities:

- Every product page has the product image on the left

- They all either use a two-column or three-column layout to display information

- The primary viewing space (above the fold) is used to display the most important key pieces of information—name, price, quantity, and product options

- Detailed product descriptions and other related products are generally separated below this area but are easily accessible to the user

By default, Magento will set our product pages to use the **2 columns with left bar** template. If, however, we need to change this for any reason, we can do so by default within our layout XML or alternatively change the layout of each product individually by following the given steps:

1. Navigate to **Catalog | Manage Products** and click on our product.
2. Within the **Design** tab, we can set **Page Layout** to either a two-column or three-column layout.

The main product area in Magento exists within the **content** block; in other words, not in the left or right column. It is within this area that we would need to focus our attention when we are deciding how to best layout our product page, especially when deciding how large our image area should be and where to place our product title, price, and add-to-cart button.

There is no true "one-size-fits-all" for layouts. Although the similarities of the results shown earlier are very common, there are many occasions when some aspects of a page may require more prominence than others. For example, on a product page where the item is medicine, it would make sense to reduce the size of our product image (perhaps a generic plastic tub of pills) and instead highlight the medical ingredients, directions for use, and possible side effects.

Optimizing our headings

The most important aspect of any landing page is that when the visitor arrives, they should be presented with a heading that relates to their original search query.

This heading should be:

- At the top of the main content area in plain sight
- Unique to the page it appears on (not duplicated on other pages)

Magento automatically populates our category page heading (an `<h1>` tag) with our category name. In most cases, this should be perfectly acceptable, but if we wanted to adjust our heading (in order to tailor it more specifically to our chosen search phrase), we would have to do so by changing our category name—this is not ideal.

Unfortunately, it is quite common for categories and products to have the same name and, therefore, the same heading. For categories, this is normally seen when double-categorizing for the sake of usability, for example as seen in the following screenshot:

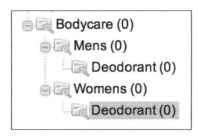

In order to resolve these issues for categories, we could:

1. Change our category structure so **Mens** and **Womens** are children of one single **Deodorant**.

2. Change our category names so that they read **Mens Deodorant** and **Womens Deodorant**.

3. Use the **Creare SEO** extension, which will provide us with a new input field so that we can edit the heading tag on each of our categories—much like with page titles (covered in *Chapter 8, Purpose-built Magento Extensions for SEO/CRO*).

For our product pages, Magento will automatically set our `<h1>` tag to our product name, so we should try to make sure that every product has a unique name. We wouldn't want to change our heading by adding in any extra keywords as the product name is exactly what our customers would expect to see on this page and is the most relevant heading.

Optimizing product and category descriptions

There are some common opinions within the SEO community about how much content we should have on an optimized page. The general consensus is that the length of the content should be appropriate to the type of page we are serving and should be relevant, unique, and engaging.

When we look back at our top five search results for "Wooden dining chairs", we will notice one important and glaringly obvious mistake: not a single one of these high-ranking pages features a dedicated category description.

So why should we bother? Well, as mentioned previously, search engines look at many aspects of a web page in order to judge how well suited it is for people searching for a particular phrase.

From our results, we can see that although they're not providing a dedicated category description, these web pages are obviously making up for lack of descriptive copy in other ways. In fact, on these websites, they have probably decided that a description would interfere with the usability of the page in some way and have therefore decided not to provide one.

Unless our website has already built up enough authority to avoid using category descriptions, it is definitely recommended to add relevant copy to our optimized category pages. We must, however, make sure that by doing so we are adhering to the following guidelines:

- The category description is unique and worthy of our visitors attention, perhaps even mentioning a notable product from a specific range
- It does not impede the visitors view of product images or other important elements on the page
- It is written for humans—not simply for search engines
- If we're struggling to write more than 100 words for our page, leave it at 100 words—at least those words will be relevant

An example of a high-ranking category page that features a category description can in fact be found within the results of our Google.com search for wooden dining chairs (just under our top five). IKEA has used the space above the product listing grid to display a brief introduction to the category, which is shown in the following screenshot:

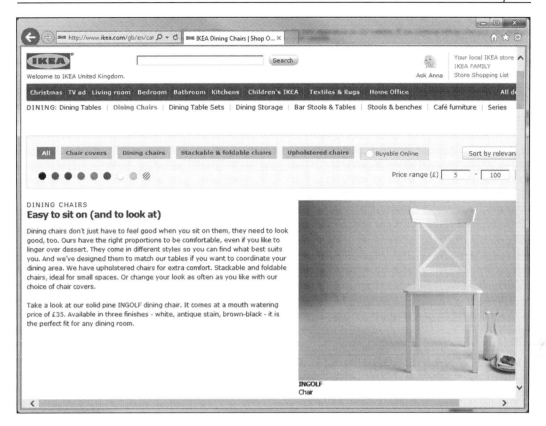

However, in this case, it would appear as though the description is in fact causing users to scroll further than necessary to get a good look at the grid of products, especially on a smaller screen size.

Product descriptions obviously need to describe the product on that specific page, and there are a few general rules to consider when writing them:

- Wherever possible, keep product descriptions unique. Do not simply copy the standard manufacturers description (this may lead to problems with duplicate content as it has undoubtedly been used on many other websites selling the same product as ours).

- Make sure that the description is well formatted and easy for the visitors to find. Try not to hide the description inside a tab (especially if this tab is not immediately visible to the user).

Additional tips for content

Within Magento, there are many other ways in which we can add relevant content to our category and product pages, such as:

- **Related products**: These are a good way of internally linking our products together and are also extremely useful for customer navigation.

- Displaying attribute information on our product pages so that our **Additional Information** section is shown.

- **Enabling product reviews**: These will help to bring unique, relevant content to our pages without having to write additional content ourselves.

Even mediocre reviews can have a positive impact on SEO rankings. As mentioned previously, good content is unique, engaging, and relevant, so don't be so quick to delete a 3/5 star review — these types of reviews will actually make our website appear more credible to our customers.

By default, Magento will show our product reviews on a separate page (for example, `http://www.mydomain.com /review/product/ list/id/132/category/25/`). Ideally, we would want to make sure that any reviews for our product are shown on our initial product page. We will cover how to do this in *Chapter 4, Template/Design Adjustments for SEO and CRO*.

Optimizing images and selling your product

The most frustrating aspect of running an online store is that it's physically impossible to personally pitch our product to each and every e-commerce visitor. It is therefore crucial that our product page contains as much persuasive material and useful information as possible.

One of the simplest and most beneficial ways to get across the sheer quality of our product is through good product photography.

The following are a few guidelines on how best to go about adding product photography to the product page:

- The main product image should be large—at least 25 percent of the main content column width

- The image should be of high quality and an option for the user to zoom-in or expand the image should be provided

- The image should be in context (for example, a wooden dining chair should be situated on the floor next to a dining table, not floating in space)

- If you provide multiple color choices, or your product comes bundled with accessories, provide an image of each

When optimizing our images, we should ensure that both the `alt` tag (alternate text) of our image and the filename (for example, `myfilename.jpg`) have been set to contain either our product name or the specific keyword that we are optimizing on this page.

To set our image alternate text, we must enter it when editing our product:

1. Navigate to **Catalog | Manage Products** and select a product.

2. Click on the **Image** tab and within **Label**, enter our chosen keyword (or product name) as shown in the following screenshot:

Image	Label	Sort Order	Thumbnail [STORE VIEW]	Small Image [STORE VIEW]	Base Image [STORE VIEW]	Exclude	Remove
No image			○	○	○		
	HTC Touch Dia	1	◉	◉	◉	✔	☐

Another massively expanding element that we find on product pages across the Internet these days are product videos. Product videos are typically short, informative, and (if done correctly) are extremely persuasive in getting across all the best aspects of our product to our customers in the shortest amount of time.

One of the best company-based videos I have seen in a long time is *Dollar Shave Club*. They advertise a single product but in such an imaginative and truly hilarious way (this may be taking it a little too far) at `goo.gl/UzcMNn`.

When it comes to writing copy for our product pages, we should think about adding personality. The more personality that goes into a product description, the more inclined a customer is to read and be affected by it. However, we must ensure that the important aspects of our product are still covered, especially when it comes down to technical data—not adding this can be a very costly mistake. For example, if we were selling a technical item such as a camera and failed to provide all the necessary information such as megapixels and zoom, a potential customer may not be sure if our product is the correct one for them. This may lead to the customer leaving our website in search of another company who has clearly listed the full product specification.

One of the most important features that we can implement on Magento product pages is customer reviews. Reviews are fast becoming vital for product pages, mainly for the following reasons:

- They provide the page with fresh content (if configured to show up on the product page itself—covered within *Chapter 4, Template/Design Adjustments for SEO and CRO*).

- They provide us with the means to use structured data markup or schema so that we can provide search engines with a user rating of our product. This rating is then used in the SERPs.

- A good rating generated by a high number of reviews quite naturally helps with a customer's buying decision about our item.

Implementing schema (rich snippets)

When visitors browse our website, they instinctively understand the meaning behind certain elements on the page. They understand when they are viewing a product page, reading reviews of our product, and even understand the difference between our recommended retail price (RRP) and our special price simply due to the layout of the page and how we have styled those elements.

Although search engines are becoming smarter every year, we can't rely on them to instinctively pinpoint the exact locations of these elements on our page. Microdata introduced with HTML5 helps to specify these elements for major search engines, such as Google, Bing, and Yahoo!.

There are a number of different canonical tag vocabularies on the Internet that are compatible with major search engines. For e-commerce, one of the better vocabularies is called *Good Relations,* and is well worth taking a look at goo.gl/4R96K9.

The main reason why we would want to implement the schema.org structured data format (aka schema) into our Magento website is to increase our **click-through rate (CTR)** in the SERPs by providing us with a rich snippet. Rich snippets are essentially special display options that Google can activate on a specific listing in the SERPs—dependant on the interpreted content of that particular web page.

When searching for Sea Foam Nail Head Parsons Chairs, we can see many types of results (randomly taken from the result page):

> 1. **Sea Foam Nail Head Parsons Chairs** (Set of 2) | Overstock.com
>   www.overstock.com › ... › Dining Room & Bar Furniture › Dining Chairs ▾
>   ★★★★★ Rating: 4.4 - 23 reviews - $129.99
>   Buy **Sea Foam Nail Head Parsons Chairs** (Set of 2) at an everyday discount price on Overstock.com! Get everyday free shipping over $50*. Read some product ...
>
> 2. **Sea Foam Nail Head Parsons Chairs** (Set of 2) - contemporary ...
>   www.houzz.com › ... › Dining Products › Dining Chairs and Benches ▾
> $129.99
>   With this set of two **sea foam** green **Parsons chairs**, you can turn your dining room ...
>   Sea Foam Nail Head Parsons Chairs (Set of 2) contemporary dining chairs ...
>
> 3. **Sea Foam Nail Head Parsons Chairs** (Set of 2), Dining Room & Bar ...
>   overstock24.net/**sea-foam-nail-head-parsons-chairs**-set-2 ▾
>   by Кира Денисова - in 3,671 Google+ circles
>   Sea Foam Nail Head Parsons Chairs (Set of 2) - Product details Update your home with this set of two Parsons ... Blue Women's 'Misha' **Tan** Print Ballet Flats.
>
> 4. **Tan Nail Head Parsons Chairs** (Set Of 2) (Tan Set Of 2 Wood ...
>   shopping.yahoo.com › ... › Kitchen & Dining Room Collections & Sets ▾
>   Shopping is the best place to comparison shop for **Tan Nail Head Parsons Chairs** ...
>   These chairs feature a dark wood finish and a **sea foam** fabric upholstery.

From the preceding screenshot, we can see three different structured data implementations and one listing without a rich snippet:

- **Listing 1**: Contains the Product, Offer, and AggregateRating schema all on one page. This allows Google to pick up on the aggregated rating of the product based on the number of reviews for that product (which is also shown) and also the current price (or price range).

- **Listing 2**: Contains only the `Product` schema; therefore, Google picks up on this and simply displays the price of the product.

- **Listing 3**: Contains authorship markup—this is to highlight the need to make certain that the structured data we are using matches the page type (this example would be appropriate, however, if the listing were a review of the product).

- **Listing 4**: Does not display any rich snippets and looks rather plain in comparison.

Although it is possible to combine several different types of structured data on any one page, many search engines will only display a single rich snippet depending on which type of structured data takes priority on the page. However, microdata within the same categorization (such as product, offer, and rating) will be combined in the SERPs to provide a more comprehensive snippet.

In our case, we would want to implement the `Product`, `Offer`, and `AggregateRating` schema onto our product pages as these type of structured data formats complement each other and will be used together.

 For more information on these schema types, please visit
`http://schema.org/`.

Adding the schema.org markup to our templates

In order to provide Google with our structured data, we must first add tags to our template file and wrap these tags around our dynamic product data.

There are many ways to insert our schema into our template files, and the following may not prove to be best practice, but for the sake of simplicity within this book, we will enter our schema in the following steps:

1. Within the `app/design/frontend/[package]/[theme]/template/catalog/product/view.phtml` file, add the following schema and custom code (highlighted):

```
<div class="product-view" itemscope
  itemtype="http://schema.org/Product">
<!-- code not shown -->
<h1 itemprop="name">[our product name code]</h1>
<!--this is our normal review block-->
<?php echo $this->getReviewsSummaryHtml($_product, false,
  true) ?>
<!-- code not shown -->
<!-- new section to add our availability and price -->
```

```php
<?php if($_product->isAvailable()): ?>
  <div class="no-display" itemprop="offers" itemscope
    itemtype="http://schema.org/Offer">
      <span itemprop="price"><?php echo
        Mage::helper('core')->currency($_product->
        getFinalPrice()) ?></span>
      <link itemprop="availability"
        href="http://schema.org/InStock" />
  </div>
<?php endif; ?>

<?php if ($_product->getShortDescription()):?>
  <!-- code not shown -->
  <div class="std" itemprop="description">[short description
    code here]</div>
  <!-- code not shown -->
<?php endif;?>
```

2. Within the `app/design/frontend/[package]/[theme]/ template/ catalog/product/view/media.phtml` file, edit both instances of the following variable to add our image into our product schema (schema highlighted):

```php
<!-- code not shown -->
  $_img = '<img itemprop="image" [rest of image code here]
<!-- code not shown -->
```

3. Within the `app/design/frontend/[package]/[theme]/ template/ review/helper/summary.phtml` file, enter the following schema and custom code (highlighted):

```php
<?php if ($this->getReviewsCount()): ?>
<div class="ratings" itemprop="aggregateRating" itemscope
  itemtype="http://schema.org/AggregateRating">
<span class="no-display" itemprop="reviewCount"><?php echo
  $this->getReviewsCount() ?> reviews</span>
<?php if ($this->getRatingSummary()):?>
<!-- code not shown -->
<!-- for % rating
<span class="no-display" itemprop="worstRating">0</span>
<span class="no-display" itemprop="bestRating">100</span>
<span class="no-display" itemprop="ratingValue"><?php echo
  $this->getRatingSummary() ?></span>
-->
<!-- for /5 star-rating -->
<span class="no-display" itemprop="worstRating">0</span>
<span class="no-display" itemprop="bestRating">5</span>
<span class="no-display" itemprop="ratingValue"><?php echo
  round($this->getRatingSummary()/20,1) ?></span>
<-- code not shown -->
```

With the ratings schema, we can specify either a percentage-based rating or an out-of-five rating. I have provided both options in the preceding code for you to use.

Once all the preceding steps are complete, we will have specified our:

- The `Product` schema consisting of the name, description, and image as well as containing:

    ° `AggregateRating`: **Which contains** `reviewcount`, `worstrating`, `bestrating`, **and** `ratingvalue`

    ° `Offer`: **Which contains** `price` **and** `availability`

We can then preview our rich snippets using the **Structured Data Testing Tool** provided by Google (`goo.gl/K6HpFg`) simply by entering our URL or HTML of our page. We should see a preview of our results listing similar to the following screenshot:

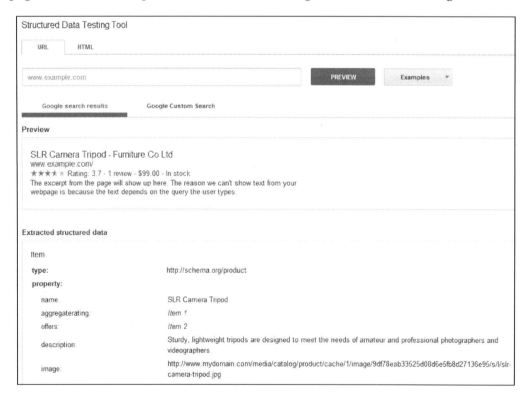

The structured data testing tool provides us with a good preview of how our listing will look no matter how many schema elements we add to our templates. It will also act as a good measure for our schemas that Google may decide to implement (for example, showing authorship over product data).

Wherever possible, schema should be entered into the HTML and rendered visibly on the page. In this instance, I have chosen to add the `AggregateRating` and `Offer` schema as hidden elements. This was to keep the editing to a minimum. When adding your own schema, it is recommended to look deeper into the code to find the specific areas to tie your schema into (for example, `catalog/product/view/type/default.phtml`—for simple product types).

Please note that rich snippets like our product schema may take up to six weeks to appear in Google. As long as the testing tool is showing the information, it means it has been applied correctly and we just have to be patient for Google to begin to display our snippets.

Implementing social sharing for products

The main aim when using social sharing buttons on a website is to allow visitors the option of sharing our page/website within their own social circle. In turn, this would lead to the possibility of other like-minded web users being made aware of and possibly visiting our website.

As shown in the preceding section, there is evidence to suggest social shares (or signals) are becoming a search engine ranking factor. The number of social shares being representative of a vote for our web page is similar to how links are treated by search engines currently.

For more information on search engine ranking factors, please see the following link (`moz.com`): `goo.gl/Rz17lo`.

There have been mixed opinions on whether or not social widgets are applicable to product pages; however, due to the release of product-specific social tags, such as Twitter product cards and Open Graph, the relevance is now clear.

With these two simple implementations, it's now easy to add an advertisement of our product when the user tweets our page or likes it on Facebook using any number of social sharing widgets—some of which we will look at in *Chapter 8, Purpose-built Magento Extensions for SEO/CRO*.

It is relatively straightforward to implement Twitter cards and the Open Graph format on our product pages; all we need to do is add some meta information to our `<head>` tag. I have written a blog post of how to integrate both of these types into our Magento product pages at `goo.gl/nTnAz8`.

When configured correctly, our product becomes a part of the users' Tweet/Like/Pin and would look similar to the following screenshot:

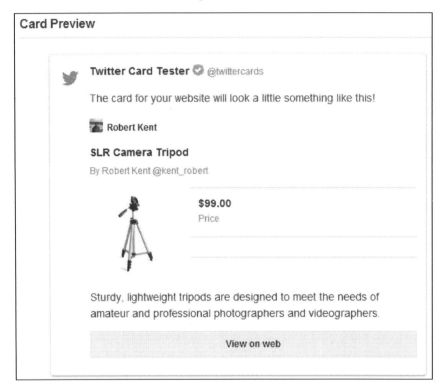

Summary

In this chapter, we have covered a lot of factors that govern how well our product and category pages can be optimized. We've looked at the general rules for setting up our page titles, descriptions, and layout, and how these differ between categories and products. We've also seen that there are many other ranking factors besides meta information that govern how high a page ranks in the SERPs.

With a few simple lines of code, it is really easy to implement product schema and social elements such as Twitter cards into our Magento templates. This is highly recommended for any e-commerce store—especially when we have enabled our reviews and ratings that help to increase our CTR within the SERPs.

3
Managing Internationalization and Multiple Languages

Magento provides us with the ability to target specific countries using its own inbuilt store management system. When a website is live on the Internet, it is accessible from almost anywhere; therefore, it is important that our website is easily findable around the world. To do this, we must be able to rank well in the search engines that reside in each of the countries we are targeting.

While preparing our website, we must be mindful of the fact that many of our category, product, and CMS pages will be duplicated across URLs. Therefore, we must learn how to make the search engines aware that we are providing these pages in multiple languages and also how to provide them with all the relevant information so that our rankings do not suffer as a result of these duplications.

In this chapter, we will be learning how to do the following:

- Choose the best URL structure to suit our multilanguage setup, understand the positives and negatives of each configuration with respect to SEO, and how to implement a subdirectory-based store structure

- Change our page titles, descriptions, and content for each store view and understand the limitations of global scope attributes

- Indicate to search engines that the content we are serving is intended for a specific language and avoid duplicate content penalties

Choosing the right domain structure for multiregional websites

When it comes to optimizing a website that targets different countries and languages, the most important rule to follow is that each translation of a page must have its own unique URL. This is to allow search engines to easily distinguish our translated pages and also to let our visitors know that they are viewing the website with a particular locale. As Magento allows us to change the base URL for each of our stores, changing the URL becomes relatively easy to execute. The only consideration would be the format in which we should be configuring our URLs.

Depending on our website setup, the general consensus is to set our base URLs to match one of the following formats:

- **ccTLD (country code Top-Level-Domain)**:
    - **Example**: `www.mydomain.fr`
    - **Positives**: Geo-targeting performed by the TLD, and easy to distinguish for customers
    - **Negatives**: It is difficult to manage multiple domain names and some ccTLDs are hard to acquire, have limited availability, and can be expensive

- Subdomains with **gTLDs (generic Top-Level-Domains)**:
    - **Example**: `fr.mydomain.com`
    - **Positives**: Geo-targetting can be performed by using Webmaster Tools and is relatively easy to set up
    - **Negatives**: Here, geo-targeting for customers may not be clearly evident and could conflict with other subdomains in-use on the domain (for example, `m.mydomain.com`)

- Subdirectories with gTLDs:
    - **Example**: `www.mydomain.com/fr/`
    - **Positives**: Geo-targetting can be performed by using Webmaster Tools, is easy to set up, and minimal cost is involved
    - **Negatives**: Here, geo-targeting for customers may not be clearly evident

For more information on optimizing the domain structure for multiregional websites, please visit the following URL (`google.com`):`goo.gl/MB9zm0`.

Depending on our website strategy, any one of these implementations could suit our needs; however, if simplicity is the main goal, I would personally recommend using subdirectories with a gTLD.

The subdirectory method will allow us to use the same administration panel without the need to perform any complicated server adjustments, such as changing our vhosts configuration. Also, by using geo-targeting within Google Webmaster Tools, we are providing Google with the same level of information that ccTLDs provide automatically.

The following steps assume that a multistore configuration has already been set up within our Magento installation. For more information on setting up multistore Magento websites, please see the following link (magentocommerce.com): http://goo.gl/iYNKO8.

In order to set up our subdirectory structure, we simply have to perform the following steps:

1. Create a new folder in our root to match our chosen language (for example, /fr/) and copy our Magento index.php and .htaccess files into it from the Magento installation root.

> On some operating systems (such as Mac OS X), .htaccess files might be hidden from view until the directory is opened in a web authoring application (such as Adobe Dreamweaver) or the "show hidden files" setting has been enabled.

2. Within the copied .htaccess file, we can specify our store code by entering the following code at the bottom of the file:

```
SetEnv MAGE_RUN_CODE fr
```

> To find our store code (in this case, fr), we can navigate to **System | Manage Stores**, click on **Store View Name** for our chosen store (for example, **French**), and look in the box labeled **Code**.

3. Within the copied index.php file, we must make sure that our paths are correct (mentioned in the previous directory) by changing the following highlighted code:

```
$compilerConfig = MAGENTO_ROOT . '/../includes/config.php';
// and
$mageFilename = MAGENTO_ROOT . '/../app/Mage.php';
```

4. Within **System | Configuration**, we can dive into our store view customization by clicking on our store view (for example, **French**) from the **Current Configuration Scope** dropdown.

5. We can then set our store-specific configuration under **Web | Unsecure** and **Web | Secure** by unchecking the **Use Website** checkbox next to each of the textboxes, as shown in the following screenshot:

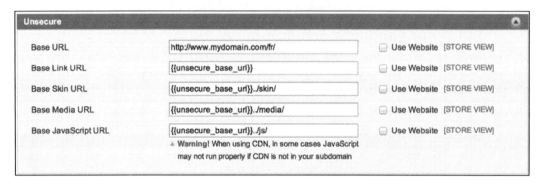

6. Within **Base URL**, we should enter our full URL path including our /fr/ subdomain, and for **Base Skin URL**, **Base Media URL**, and **Base JavaScript URL**, we should add ../ to our path in order to fetch the files from outside our /fr/ directory (for example, {{unsecure_base_url}}../js/).

7. We can then click on **Save Config** and navigate to our new store in the new subdirectory, for example, www.mydomain.com/fr/.

Then, in order to set up geo-targeting for our new subdirectory, we can simply perform the following steps:

1. Log in to Google Webmaster Tools (http://www.google.com/webmasters) and click on **Add a site**; enter our new URL including the subdirectory, as shown in the following screenshot:

2. After verifying the domain, we can click on this site and then on the settings button (top right); here, click on **Site Settings**. At the top, we can specify **Geographic Target**.

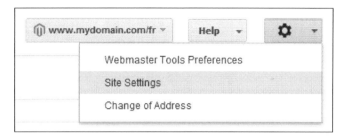

Store-specific configuration

> *"Google only uses the visible content of your page to determine its language."*
>
> *-Google*

It is important to make sure that we translate as much as possible when providing users with translated versions of our product, category, and CMS pages. We can translate manually entered text by manipulating the values on a per-store scope configuration level within the administration panel as follows:

- For categories, we should navigate to **System | Manage Categories** and select our store from the **Choose Store View** dropdown (as shown in the following screenshot). We should then translate our values for **Name**, **Description**, **Page Title**, and **Meta Description**.

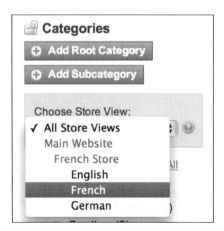

- For products, we should navigate to **System | Manage Products**, click on our product, and then select our store from the **Choose Store View** dropdown. We should then change our **Name**, **Description**, **Short Description**, and **Meta Information** values where appropriate.

- For pages, we would need to create additional CMS pages and then select the appropriate store view within **Page Information | Store View**. We can then enter our translated **Content**, **Meta Information**, **Page Title**, and even **URL Key** values.

Translating URL keys

URL keys for products can be changed on a per-store basis so long as we change the **Scope** of the attribute to **Store View** rather than **Global**. To do this, we would need to navigate to **Catalog | Attributes | Manage Attributes**, click on the **url_key** attribute, and change the **Scope** to **Store View**, as shown in the following screenshot:

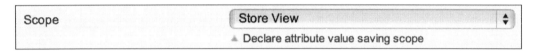

>
> Unfortunately, by default, Magento does not allow category URLs to be configured per-store scope, which is a definite problem when we want to translate them into different languages.
>
> Hopefully, newer versions of Magento will feature store-scope category URL keys. For now there is a hack, but please be aware that it is a hack and use it only on your development environment until you are sure there are no adverse effects. To find the hack, please visit the following URL: goo.gl/YPrmyJ

Translating template content

There are a few methods to translate the text that is embedded within the template files (text that we cannot edit via the administration panel, for example, the Add to Cart button label, and so on). The most popular is to install a language pack or locale. To do this, we would perform the following steps:

1. Visit www.magentocommerce.com/translations, download the relevant language pack, and install the files in the applicable directories.

2. Within **System | Configuration | General**, set **Locale** to our downloaded language, making sure our **Current Configuration Scope** is set to the store we wish to apply the translations on.

We can also translate text through our own theme locale folders using a file called `translate.csv`. For more information on how to do this, please visit the following link (`tomrobertshaw.net`): `goo.gl/zD5ECW`.

As Google and other search engines pick up on a variety of elements on the page, it's important to try to translate as many configuration options as possible. Here are a few important areas to consider:

- Default store information (**System | Configuration | General | Store Information**), especially address and phone number if available

- Product attribute values/labels (**Catalog | Attributes | Manage Attributes**); these can be edited per store as long as the **Scope** is set to **Store View**

- For translations not covered by the language pack, we can use the Translate Inline tool (**System | Configuration | Developer | Translate Inline**) and set **Enabled for Frontend** to **Yes**

For a complete tutorial on using Translate Inline, please see the following link (`inchoo.net`): `goo.gl/VaQkY0`.

It is extremely important that, when adding translations to our websites, we hire a translator who is native to that particular country. The copy must then be optimized for SEO, just as it would when writing it ourselves.

We must pay particularly close attention to the translation of our keywords. These are our most important phrases and must be translated correctly for the appropriate search engine and audience.

Avoiding duplicate content when translating pages

While translating our Magento store, we can never be too careful when it comes to duplicate content. Essentially, what we are doing is duplicating our Magento installation and then translating the same pages into different languages.

In order to specifically inform search engines such as Google and Yandex of the locations of our translated pages, we should use the `rel="alternate"` `hreflang="x"` tag.

This tag lets search engines know the exact location and intended audience of our translated pages. There are two implementations of this tag; one is with meta information stored in the `<head>` tag per page and the other is through the XML sitemap.

The correct method for using the `rel="alternate" hreflang="x"` tag is to include a copy of it within our `<head>` area for each and every translated version of our page. The following is an example of that:

```
<-- default to our primary website language version of this page
   using x-default -->
<link rel="alternate" hreflang="x-default" href=
   "http://www.mydomain.com/my-product.html" />
<link rel="alternate" hreflang="fr" href=
   "http://www.mydomain.com/fr/my-product.html" />
```

Here, `hreflang` can either be a standard ISO 639-1 code (language classification) or alternatively appended with an ISO 3166-1 alpha-2 code (country code). In fact, we could let search engines know about a page that targets a language in a specific country, for example, `fr-ca` for French-speaking Canadians.

In this instance, it would be appropriate to name our folder structure in the same way so that we can create a specific store view for French speaking Canadians—for example, `/fr-ca/`—so that we can set the correct currency, and so on.

For a detailed list of possible ISO-format country codes, please see the following URL (`iso.org`): `goo.gl/5HPp5g`.

The XML sitemap method, however, is the preferred way of informing search engines about multiple languages on our website, and a good example of this can be found on the `store.apple.com` website. We can see that they cater to many countries (also using the subdirectory method) within their own XML sitemap:

```
<urlset xmlns="http://www.sitemaps.org/schemas/sitemap/
   0.9"  xmlns:xhtml="http://www.w3.org/1999/xhtml">
<url>
<loc>http://store.apple.com/us/browse/home/shop_mac</loc>
<xhtml:link rel="alternate" hreflang="en-us" href=
   "http://store.apple.com/us/browse/home/shop_mac" />
<xhtml:link rel="alternate" hreflang="en-ae" href=
   "http://store.apple.com/ae/browse/home/shop_mac" />

<!-- another 40 combinations for this url not shown -->
```

At this moment, it is unclear as to whether there is a Magento extension available that will provide us with either the `<head>` implementation or the XML sitemap version in the correct format, and doing this manually could take a very long time (depending on the complexity of our website).

For now, we can implement a standard set of tags within our Magento website that (although not perfect) will provide search engines with at least a modicum of knowledge about the available translations on our website. To do this, we should add our tags by navigating to **System | Configuration | Design | HTML Head | Miscellaneous Scripts** (simply the base URLs), as shown in the following screenshot:

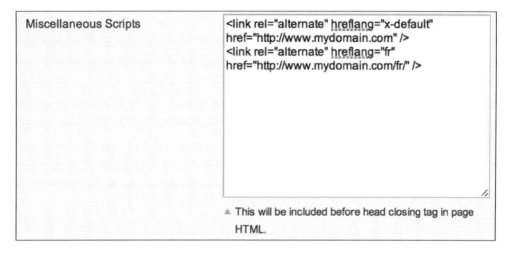

For more information on what the `rel="alternate" hreflang="x"` tag can do, please see the following link (`google.com`): `goo.gl/Bk47LE`.

Summary

In this chapter, we have learned about the different ways in which we can structure the domains/URLs of our different store views in order to cater to different languages as well as looked at an example of how to set up the subdirectory method. From this, we have seen how we can change our configuration scope to adjust certain elements on our pages, such as titles, descriptions, and (some) URL keys.

We've installed a language pack on our French store view and also looked at other important areas/methods for translations.

We now understand the importance of the `rel="alternate" hreflang="x"` tag within our Magento store and can implement a short-term fix (unless a lot of hard work is achieved through XML sitemap generation or manual addition into the template) until an extension or update within Magento enables this feature dynamically for us.

Now that our multilanguage store has been set up correctly, in *Chapter 4, Template/ Design Adjustments for SEO and CRO*, we can begin to look at modifying our Magento template files for products and categories in order to better optimize their content for both search engines and customers.

4
Template/Design Adjustments for SEO and CRO

Magento allows us to edit any part of a theme using template files, layout XML files, and, of course, **CSS (cascading style sheet)** files. There are hundreds of free and premium themes available on the Internet and they each have their own take on template page optimization. For the basis of this chapter, we will be concentrating on the Magento base theme, and how we can improve the template markup to better structure our content for SEO and **CRO (conversion rate optimization)**.

Most third-party themes tend to structure their templates on the base theme, so we may see similarities between the code shown here and the code within any custom/downloaded theme that we may have installed.

Magento has evolved rapidly since Version 1.3 back in 2009-2010, especially through changes to the default theme. Where possible, I will try to describe a few major SEO-related problems that exist within these earlier versions and how to fix them.

In this chapter, we will be looking at the following points:

- How to organize our heading structure (h1, h2, h3) and where to change these in our template files
- How to integrate other types of schema such as the `breadcrumb` schema into our templates
- How to optimize our category pagination and how to add reviews directly onto our product pages
- The main points to consider when streamlining our customer journey through our Magento website

Organizing our heading structure

A good heading structure is important for any website; not only does it clearly define the page structure for search engines, but it also plays a vital role in user accessibility.

 Screen readers use our page's heading tags to allow a visually impaired user quick access to certain sections of our page. See the following post about how accessibility features can benefit SEO (webaim.org): goo.gl/YaI5nl.

It is recommended to have only one instance of an `<h1>` tag on each page; this is to describe the overall purpose of the page. Other heading types such as `<h2>`, `<h3>`, and so on can occur multiple times on the same page as they describe the different levels or subsections within that page.

It is also a best practice to ensure `<h1>` tags are unique across the website as a whole. As mentioned previously, these are used to define the subject matter of the page. If multiple pages have the same `<h1>` tag, we are essentially telling search engines that these two pages serve the same purpose. A well-structured website should contain pages that are unique in both purpose and content.

Changing our heading structure on the home, category, and product pages

In my opinion, Magento CE 1.3 was a definitive release and really sparked the rising interest in the Magento platform. There is however a major issue with regards to the heading structure within Magento CE 1.3, and that is the fact that our `<h1>` tag is always preset for us within the header of our website and is not editable within the CMS.

The adverse effect of this is that each of our web pages will contain the same primary heading tag. Search engines and screen readers alike may get confused when browsing our website, and this will almost certainly result in a negative impact on our rankings.

As mentioned in previous chapters, we should always try our best to make sure that our headings (especially `<h1>` and ideally `<h2>`) are unique on every single page of our Magento store.

In order to remedy this issue in Magento 1.3, within `app/design/frontend/`
`[package]/[theme]/template/page/html/header.phtml`:

- Change `<h1 id="logo">` to `<span id="logo">` and adjust our
  CSS accordingly

- Alternatively, take the approach that was introduced with Magento CE 1.4
  and conditionally implement `<h1>` within our `header.phtml` file for the
  home page only (shown as follows).

From Magento CE 1.4 to Magento CE 1.8, we will see that our `header.phtml` file has
been adjusted to only show `<h1>` with our logo (and all important alternative text) on
our home page using the following conditional code:

```php
<?php if ($this->getIsHomePage()):?>
  <h1 class="logo"><!-- our image code here --></h1>
<?php else:?>
  <!—image without the <h1> tag -->
<?php endif?>
```

Unfortunately, Magento CE 1.3 doesn't come equipped with the `$this-`
`>getIsHomePage()` method; however, we can use other alternative methods on our
page to get the desired result (`goo.gl/EmZVFx`).

From the preceding code, we can see that Magento already attempts to optimize the
heading on our home page to match our brand (website logo and alternative text).
As mentioned in *Chapter 1, Preparing and Configuring Your Magento Website*, it is best
practice to optimize each page for the keywords that are most relevant.

Once this has been set up successfully, we can now use our `<h1>` tag within our
other templates without worrying about there being multiple `<h1>` tags on each page
(although this is acceptable within HTML5 markup), and we can now implement
best practice for headings on our category and product pages.

For categories:

- Our main category heading (by default the name of our category) should be
  within an `<h1>` tag (in Version 1.3, we should swap this from `<h2>` within
  `.../[theme]/template/catalog/category/view.phtml`)

- If we are listing products on our category pages, our product names should
  be relegated to the `<h3>` or `<h4>` tags (found within `.../[theme]/template/`
  `catalog/product/list.phtml`); this will free up our `<h2>` tag so that if
  we were writing a category description, we could insert another prominent
  heading into the page

For products:

- Our product name should be within an `<h1>` tag (again, Magento 1.3, due to already setting an `<h1>` tag, will have made our product name `<h3>`; we can change this within . . . / [theme] /template/catalog/product/view.phtml)
- Additional information or a product description heading should be set to `<h2>`
- Any related product names should be set to `<h3>`

It is important to stress that when deciding on a heading structure, we must try to maintain relevance wherever possible. We should be thinking about the page as a whole; what sections within that page require headings, and what their hierarchy should be in terms of importance for search engines and most importantly our users.

Some versions of Magento (mainly versions before Magento CE 1.4) also tend to overuse heading tags, so we should try wherever possible to trim down our headings (by replacing them with `<span>` tags) in our templates. Here are a few places to check:

- Left/right column block headings (such as the My Cart block, typically found within . . . / [theme] /template/checkout/cart/sidebar.phtml in Magento CE 1.3)
- Product page `<h4>` elements, such as More Views (typically found within . . . / [theme] /template/catalog/product/view/media.phtml)

A useful tip for figuring out your heading structure is to use a browser plugin like Web Developer Tools for Chrome (goo.gl/ihPJnP), where you can simply click on a button within the **Information** tab called **View Document Outline**. This will display your heading structure like this:

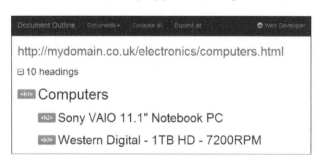

Integrating the breadcrumb and organization schema

Along with the `Product` and `Review` schemas, which we looked at in *Chapter 2, Product and Category Page Optimization*, there are many other schema types that we can implement within our template files. In this section, we will look at implementing the following:

- The `breadcrumb` rich snippet
- The `organization` (aka `logo`) schema

Adding structured data to our breadcrumbs

The `breadcrumb` rich snippet is highly recommended for any e-commerce website as it helps to improve the legibility of our URL within the SERPs. Along with this, it provides the user with multiple links under the result to give that user the option to visit our category pages directly from the search engine.

Search engines such as Google can recognize the breadcrumb structure on our pages and will use these to create rich snippets within the SERPs. For example, if we were to take a look at three results from our `wooden dining chairs` search term, we would see some interesting results:

A few interesting points to consider here are:

- The Amazon listing does not display breadcrumbs
- The Overstock listing uses the `breadcrumb` rich snippet, and these are displayed in the SERPs
- The Wayfair listing does not use the `breadcrumb` rich snippet but breadcrumbs are displayed nonetheless

Although breadcrumb structured data is a great way to explicitly state how our breadcrumbs should appear, smart search engines such as Google will pick up on other factors (such as a set of delimited links that accurately reflect the site hierarchy) to dynamically insert breadcrumbs into the SERPs.

In order to implement breadcrumbs using RDF (rich data format) into our template files, we would need to open up `app/design/frontend/[package]/[theme]/template/page/html/breadcrumbs.phtml` and edit the following code (highlighted):

```php
<?php if($crumbs && is_array($crumbs)): ?>
    <div class="breadcrumbs" xmlns:v="http://rdf.data-
    vocabulary.org/#">
    <ul>
        <?php foreach($crumbs as $_crumbName=>$_crumbInfo): ?>
            <li class="<?php echo $_crumbName ?>"
            typeof="v:Breadcrumb">
            <?php if($_crumbInfo['link']): ?>
            <a href="<?php echo $_crumbInfo['link'] ?>" rel="v:url"
                property="v:title" title="<?php echo $this-
                >htmlEscape($_crumbInfo['title']) ?>"><?php echo
                $this->htmlEscape($_crumbInfo['label']) ?></a>
            <!-- other conditional statements -->
            </li>
        <?php endforeach; ?>
    </ul>
    </div>
<?php endif; ?>
```

In order to add our `organization` schema around our logo, we should open up `app/design/frontend/[package]/[theme]/template/page/header.phtml` and edit the following code (highlighted):

```php
<div itemscope itemtype="http://schema.org/Organization">
    <?php if ($this->getIsHomePage()):?>
        <h1 class="logo"><strong><?php echo $this->getLogoAlt()
            ?></strong><a itemprop="url" href="<?php echo $this-
            >getUrl('') ?>" title="<?php echo $this->getLogoAlt() ?>"
            class="logo"><img itemprop="logo" src="<?php echo $this-
            >getLogoSrc() ?>" alt="<?php echo $this->getLogoAlt() ?>"
            /></a></h1>
    <?php else:?>
        <a itemprop="url" href="<?php echo $this->getUrl('') ?>"
            title="<?php echo $this->getLogoAlt() ?>"
            class="logo"><strong><?php echo $this->getLogoAlt()
            ?></strong><img itemprop="logo" src="<?php echo $this-
```

```
    >getLogoSrc() ?>" alt="<?php echo $this->getLogoAlt() ?>"
    /></a>
  <?php endif?>
</div>
```

The `organization` schema will let search engines such as Google know which logo we want to be shown when our website information is used in the SERPs.

There are many types of schema available, and a few others that may be appropriate for our Magento website are:

- **LocalBusiness schema**: This schema would be useful if we were running an online store but will also provide services within a local area
- **PostalAddress schema**: This schema type is used to mark up company address details and is useful for Contact Us/About Us pages

As mentioned within *Chapter 2, Product and Category Page Optimization*, search engines such as Google will serve the most appropriate rich snippets for our different page types.

Therefore, we can assume that the schema we introduced to our product page (`Review`, `Offer`, and `Product` schema) will either be implemented alongside our `breadcrumb` and `organization` schema or (more likely) our product-based schema will take precedence.

Adding rel=next/prev to our category pagination

Although we should set our category pages to display a canonical tag, we can also implement another feature to declare to search engines our next and previous pages when search spiders are crawling our paginated product listings.

Much like the canonical tag, this markup is aimed at letting search engines know that the pages being displayed are not meant to be interpreted as duplicate content but are instead intended to help customers navigate between lists of items.

There are a few ways to implement this code into our templates, but the most common is to add our next and previous elements only on our category pages and within the `<head>` tag.

A good tutorial on how to implement these next and previous elements can be found at the following link (inchoo): `goo.gl/PbOFhc`.

 I would recommend adapting this technique and incorporating it into layout XML and its own template file rather than pasting it directly into `head.phtml`.

Once implemented, the code should activate when viewing a category with multiple pages and should appear within the page source similar to the following:

```
<link rel="prev"
  href="http://www.mydomain.com/electronics/computers.html?p=2" />
<link rel="next"
  href="http://www.mydomain.com/electronics/computers.html?p=4" />
```

These elements will change depending on which page within the pagination we are currently viewing.

 For more information on the `<link rel="next/prev">` element and how it can work alongside our canonical tag, please see the following post (`google.com`): `goo.gl/cZrssv`.

Adding reviews directly onto our product pages

As mentioned in previous chapters, it's important that we make the most out of user-generated content. The best way to do this on our product pages is to display our reviews directly on the page (much like `amazon.com`).

By doing this, we will be adding fresh content to our product pages as well as providing useful information to our customers and increasing their likelihood to purchase our product (as long as the review is not too terrible).

To do this, we must edit our `local.xml` file once again (`.../[theme]/layout/local.xml`) and insert the following code:

```
<catalog_product_view>
  <reference name="product.info">
    <block type="review/product_view_list"
      name="product.info.product_additional_data" as="reviews"
      template="review/product/view/list.phtml">
      <action
        method="addToParentGroup">
```

```
        <group>detailed_info</group></action>
      <block type="review/form" name="product.review.form"
        as="review_form"/>
    </block>
  </reference>
</catalog_product_view>
```

This should add our reviews to our product page as well as bring out the form for other users to submit reviews. In the default or base theme, it should look like the following screenshot:

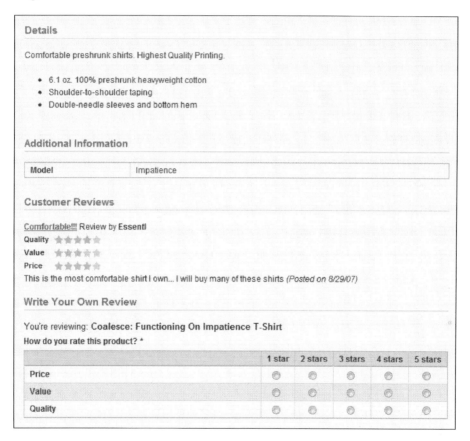

Depending on your own theme, you may wish to remove the line `<action method="addToParentGroup"><group>detailed_info</group></action>`, which groups the reviews into the additional information section.

In order to avoid duplicate content issues, we'd generally want to disable the dedicated review pages from being indexed by search engines. We can do this via `robots.txt`, which will be covered in *Chapter 7, Technical Rewrites for Search Engines*.

Interestingly, within Magento 2 (currently under development), there is a theme called Plushe.

Within this theme, the reviews that are added against a product are automatically displayed on the product page within a **Reviews** tab underneath the review entry form, just like we've performed for Magento CE 1.x.

Removing unwanted blocks from the checkout

Although not necessarily an SEO factor, we should look at a few simple techniques to optimize the Magento checkout process so that the increased traffic we are receiving has the best chance of converting into sales.

As mentioned previously, the primary goal for optimizing our Magento store should be to increase sales; once we have a steady flow of visitors to our website, we should practice CRO (conversion rate optimization) in order to maximize the chances of a customer purchasing a product.

For an excellent breakdown of common e-commerce CRO factors, please take a look at the following Holy Grail on moz.com: goo.gl/NeuFq3.

When we are talking about distractions on the checkout, we are talking about any feature that may take our customer away from the payment page. The last thing we want is for all of our hard work in getting a customer to the checkout to be wasted when they decide to browse another category and then never return to pay for their shopping cart.

By default, Magento will contain various blocks in the header and footer that can be removed on the checkout page. Elements such as the menu navigation, search box, and even top links could be removed to simplify the page and remove distractions from the main checkout process. To remove these items, we would use our local.xml file and enter the following code:

```
<checkout_cart_index>
  <reference name="header">
    <remove name="top.search" />
    <remove name="top.links" />
    <remove name="top.menu" />
  </reference>
```

```
    </checkout_cart_index>
    <checkout_onepage_index>
      <reference name="header">
        <remove name="top.search" />
        <remove name="top.links" />
        <remove name="top.menu" />
      </reference>
    </checkout_onepage_index>
```

The following image shows the effect this code can have on the look and feel of the checkout:

The effect is even more pronounced when there are custom blocks taking up a lot of space within the header/footer area. Removing these items keeps the focus of the page on the checkout form itself and not on the other elements of the page.

 We'll be looking at other checkout optimization methods in *Chapter 8, Purpose-built Magento Extensions for SEO/CRO*.

Summary

In this section, we have looked at headings, how they should be prioritized on each of the different page types, and how to fix some glaring SEO mistakes in earlier versions of Magento. We've also looked at how to implement different types of schema into different sections of our template files such as the `breadcrumb` schema and the `organization` schema (`logo`).

We've seen how easy it is to display product reviews on our product pages (rather than on a separate page) in order to continuously generate relevant, unique content on our pages to help with SEO, and we've also seen how we can remove elements from our layout in order to simplify the sales process for our customers.

In the next chapter, we will be looking at ways in which we can improve the load speed of our Magento website for the benefit of our users and also search engines, which take loading times into consideration within their ranking algorithms.

Speeding Up Your Magento Website

By default, Magento is certainly not the fastest platform in the world, but there are numerous ways available to help speed up the loading time of its pages. Magento provides us with a selection of methods through its own configuration, and we can save time off our load speed by enabling those features.

Search engines such as Google take load speed into account as a ranking factor. It is therefore extremely important that we optimize our Magento website for speed as much as possible.

In this chapter, we will learn about:

- The SEO and **user experience (UX)** benefits of serving a fast website to our visitors
- The default options that Magento comes equipped with to help with load speed
- Quick and easy `.htaccess` file modifications to leverage caching and file compression
- How we can dramatically improve the load speed of our pages through the use of dedicated caching modules
- The tools available to us to test the speed of our pages and our Magento framework

SEO benefits of a fast Magento website

As of early 2010, Google announced that it was taking into account website speed as a ranking factor. Although not necessarily a major factor, a slow website does have knock-on effects for many other algorithmic elements associated with user experience.

With the increase in computer hardware and connection speed, many Internet users now find slow-loading websites intolerable as they are becoming more and more used to receiving the information they require almost instantaneously.

The most recent statistics indicate that a page load speed of anything above 2 seconds can lead to:

- An increase in bounce rate (a visitor immediately leaving the page)
- A reduction in average time on site
- Lower website conversions

This final point is particularly worrying for us as a decrease in conversions translates into a loss in sales through our Magento store!

Google (and other search engines) understands the impact that the speed of a website has on visitors. Their primary goal is to provide value to their own users, and there is little value on offer if our visitors become frustrated and leave our website after waiting 5 to 10 seconds for a single page to load.

A fast Magento website would help to retain customers on our pages, maximizing the probability of our visitors becoming paying customers.

 Google especially welcomes fast-loading websites, so much so that there is a whole section within the Google Developers website dedicated to making the Web faster: goo.gl/4Rh2VK.

Magento configuration settings to increase speed

As Magento is such a large framework (currently well over 12,000 files in a fresh Magento CE 1.8 installation), the developers decided early on to introduce some basic features to help speed up the rendering time of its many pages. The simplest feature to implement on any Magento website is cache.

 Magento EE comes equipped with the **Full Page Cache** (FPC) module, which is a much improved version of the standard cache I'm about to show you. Magento released a whitepaper detailing the performance and scalability of EE 1.11 which contains a large section on FPC: goo.gl/R2WFkX.

To enable the Magento cache, we perform the following steps:

1. Navigate to **System | Cache Management**.

2. Click on **Select All** of our **Cache Types** option and choose **Enable** from the **Actions** drop-down menu.

3. Once we click on **Submit,** our cache should be enabled for all of the default Magento cache types. The resulting page should look similar to the following screenshot:

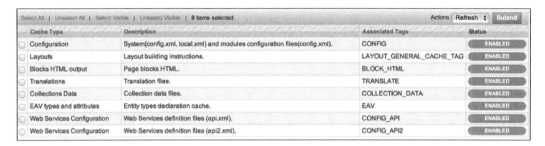

Cache Type	Description	Associated Tags	Status
Configuration	System(config.xml, local.xml) and modules configuration files(config.xml).	CONFIG	ENABLED
Layouts	Layout building instructions.	LAYOUT_GENERAL_CACHE_TAG	ENABLED
Blocks HTML output	Page blocks HTML.	BLOCK_HTML	ENABLED
Translations	Translation files.	TRANSLATE	ENABLED
Collections Data	Collection data files.	COLLECTION_DATA	ENABLED
EAV types and attributes	Entity types declaration cache.	EAV	ENABLED
Web Services Configuration	Web Services definition files (api.xml).	CONFIG_API	ENABLED
Web Services Configuration	Web Services definition files (api2.xml).	CONFIG_API2	ENABLED

There is typically an increase of 20 to 40 percent in website speed once the system cache has been enabled.

Some versions of Magento (especially CE 1.3) may look slightly different to the preceding screenshot, and certain options may not be available. However, we should make sure that we enable all cache options irrespective of which version of Magento we are using.

The following two options (compilation and merging CSS/JS) are recommended, but it is highly advisable to initially enable both of these options on your development environment as sometimes problems do occur (depending on third-party extensions).

It is also recommended to disable compilation before installing extensions.

Magento compilation speeds up the time it takes for the server to process the code base by copying all of the required PHP files into a much simpler directory structure. This allows the server to bypass a lot of directory-based navigation to find and load the required classes.

To enable Magento compilation, we will navigate to **System | Tools | Compilation** and click on **Run Compilation Process**.

The primary goal of the compiler tool is to reduce the time it takes to build our page excluding elements like images, JavaScript, and CSS. Usually, we would see a decrease in the time it takes to render the resulting HTML by approximately 200 to 400 milliseconds depending on the speed of the server.

The last simple configuration option we will discuss in this section is the merging of our JavaScript and CSS files. The primary purpose of this option is to reduce the number of requests on our web page. Typically, Magento will contain around three to four stylesheets and (depending on the page in question) around 13 JavaScript files.

Although not an inherent feature within Magento, minification (the act of compressing the content of a file into a simplified version of the same text without losing functionality) is a recommended practice for every type of website, and is especially useful for JavaScript files.

For more information on minifying JavaScript and a tool on how to perform minification, please go to www.jscompress.com.

When we merge JS and CSS, we will reduce this number to one stylesheet and one JavaScript file. This remains true for any additional custom CSS or JS file that we add through our layout XML.

To enable CSS/JS merging, we perform the following steps:

1. Navigate to **System | Configuration | Developer**.
2. Under **JavaScript Settings**, set **Merge JavaScript Files** to **Yes**, under **CSS Settings**, set **Merge CSS Files** to **Yes,** and then click on **Save Config**.

For a test case of these default configuration options affecting load time, please see the following blog post (creare.co.uk): goo.gl/c8arxs.

.htaccess modifications

The .htaccess files allow developers to make server configuration changes on a per-directory basis. Magento comes packaged with many .htaccess files, but the one which we will be dealing with in this section is the .htaccess file found on the root of our installation. As mentioned previously, in order to edit our .htaccess file, we must make sure that the web editor we are using can see the hidden files.

The most basic of performance-based .htaccess tweaks that we can make are implementing Content-Encoding (mod_deflate/mod_gzip) and Expiration Headers (mod_expires).

The gzip compression essentially presents the browser with a zipped version of the file. Compressing the file before transferring it reduces the download time required. We should add the following lines of code to our root .htaccess file in order to use these methods (if available on the server):

```
<IfModule mod_deflate.c>
  SetOutputFilter DEFLATE
  BrowserMatch ^Mozilla/4 gzip-only-text/html
  BrowserMatch ^Mozilla/4\.0[678] no-gzip
  BrowserMatch \bMSIE !no-gzip !gzip-only-text/html
  SetEnvIfNoCase Request_URI \.(?:gif|jpe?g|png)$ no-gzip dont-vary
  Header append Vary User-Agent env=!dont-vary
</IfModule>

<ifModule mod_gzip.c>
  mod_gzip_on Yes
  mod_gzip_dechunk Yes
  mod_gzip_item_include file \.(html?|txt|css|js|php|pl)$
  mod_gzip_item_include handler ^cgi-script$
  mod_gzip_item_include mime ^text/.*
  mod_gzip_item_include mime ^application/x-javascript.*
  mod_gzip_item_exclude mime ^image/.*
  mod_gzip_item_exclude rspheader ^Content-Encoding:.*gzip.*
</ifModule>
```

The `<ifModule>` tags will activate our configuration if the server has the correct module installed. We've added both the `mod_deflate` and `mod_gzip` configurations; however, you can choose to use one or the other in your own `.htaccess` file.

The next step is to set up our expiration headers, which will tell the browser to use its own cached version of our file if the expiration date of the current file is in the future. This will also reduce the download time for our users. Refer to the following code snippet:

```
<ifModule mod_expires.c>
  ExpiresActive On
  ExpiresDefault "access plus 1 seconds"
  ExpiresByType text/html "access plus 1 seconds"
  ExpiresByType image/gif "access plus 2592000 seconds"
  ExpiresByType image/jpeg "access plus 2592000 seconds"
  ExpiresByType image/png "access plus 2592000 seconds"
  ExpiresByType text/css "access plus 604800 seconds"
  ExpiresByType text/javascript "access plus 216000 seconds"
  ExpiresByType application/x-javascript "access plus 216000
    seconds"
</ifModule>
```

The time in seconds sets the future expiration date for that certain type of file. On a correctly-configured server, just by adding these few lines of code, we can reduce the loading time of a standard Magento CE 1.8 installation on average anywhere between 0.5 to 1 whole second.

It is recommended to add the `mod_expires` code to our
`.htaccess` file only after we have finished our development;
otherwise, changes to CSS/JS files may not be seen by repeated
users until they clear their browser cache.

Server-side performance and scalability

There is really only so much we can do with `.htaccess` tweaks and Magento's default
configuration to speed up the loading of our web pages. Typically speaking, the faster
and more powerful the server, the quicker our pages are rendered. There are many
different types of servers available, but for Magento websites, the best performance
can be gained through either dedicated hosting or super-fast cloud-based servers.

A hosting provider with experience hosting Magento websites
should be aware of the resource implications and the variety of
additional server extensions that are required as mentioned in
Magento's own system requirements (`magento.com`): `goo.gl/`
`Ayd1gE`.

However, the most drastic improvements can be seen through the installation and
configuration of specific web application accelerators.

One increasingly popular HTTP accelerator is **Varnish Cache**. This caching method
has been talked about a lot in web conferences around the world, and has been used
to great effect when installed alongside Magento.

In short, Varnish stores a version of the fully rendered page the first time any user
visits that particular page. The cached version is then returned to subsequent users
rather than Magento having to compile all of that data again. The result is consistent;
less than 1 second load time for the remainder of the cache lifetime.

Here are several bold claims made by the Varnish team, all of which I have yet to
see any reason to disbelieve:

- Up to 250 times faster than a default Magento installation
- Allows for incredible scalability while reducing hardware costs

For more information on Varnish Cache and Magento, please see
the following link (`varnish-software.com`): `goo.gl/PyhmVD`.

There are also other alternative caching methods available that are worth considering. The most commonly used are:

- **Redis**: This is an in-memory, key-value data store. For more information on how to configure it with Magento, please see the following link (`magentocommerce.com`): `goo.gl/mqEgpI`.

- **Memcached**: This caches data and objects in RAM to reduce the load on the database (or other external calls). For a detailed guide on how to install memcached and **alternative PHP cache** (**APC**), and how to configure them with Magento, please see the following link: `goo.gl/Ulqb4k`.

 It is possible to combine different cache types, such as memcached and Varnish, in order to speed up front end loading speed and database-driven content. However, it's important to look into each third-party application closely and determine that they will work correctly alongside each other.

Additionally, **content delivery networks** (**CDNs**) can be used to offset the traffic from our server for various files on our website. Apart from this, the user's geographical location is used to determine the closest server to them in order to provide the content.

The typical usage of a content delivery network on a Magento website would be to serve the many JavaScript files, CSS files, and product images directly from the CDN rather than our own server, improving speed and sharing the loading of these large files across several servers.

Online tools to test performance

Of course, when we are optimizing the performance of our Magento website, we must make sure that we are analyzing the speed variations so that we know that our efforts have a positive effect.

There are many page-speed testing tools out there, but a few of the best (particularly for Magento-powered websites) are:

- Mage Speed Test
- Pingdom Website Speed Test
- Google Page Speed Insights

Mage Speed Test

This tool, written by Ashley Schroder, is specifically targeted towards Magento-powered websites. It takes `sitemap.xml` from our Magento store and through a few simple settings, will measure how many times the server is successfully hit by fake users within a certain time frame.

The returned results are in the format of transactions per second (this is measured in web transactions, not Magento sales transactions) and ideally, the higher the number of users per second, the better.

You can try out the tool yourself by visiting `www.magespeedtest.com`.

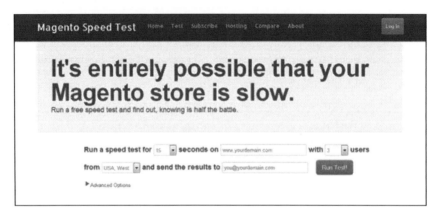

Pingdom Website Speed Test

Located at `tools.pingdom.com`, this tool is one of my favorites, and it analyzes the speed of any web page as well as gives insights into how the code on the page could be further improved. As you can see from the following screenshot, they also provide a score of our website based on their own on-page speed optimization factors:

Google Page Speed Insights

It's always smart to first listen to the people who are judging our website speed and then deciding on how to rank our website in its SERPs. The Google Page Speed Insights tool can be added as an extension to our browsers (Chrome/Firefox) or performed online through their website (goo.gl/P4wUI1).

Once ran, it will give us a score out of 100 for both mobile (when ran online) and desktop versions of our website. It also provides a fantastic list of technical changes that could be made in order to speed up the web page, prioritized as urgent, for consideration, and factors that we have already implemented. The following screenshot shows the results shown inside the Google Chrome extension:

Summary

In this chapter, we have looked at how search engines such as Google interpret page speed within their ranking algorithms. We've also looked at the importance of the user experience factor and how websites that take longer than 2 seconds to load could affect our website's conversions (sales).

We've seen that Magento comes equipped with several options directed at improving the performance of our website and also looked at several tweaks that we can make to our .htaccess file in order to further improve our load speeds.

There are many page-speed-specific modules available that we can implement onto our servers to dramatically affect loading times, Varnish Cache being one of the most popular implementations in recent times.

Making changes such as these means nothing without the ability to test our page speeds, so we have also taken a look at some of the most popular page-speed tools available. Many of which provide additional information that further help us to adapt the way we structure the content of our pages and configure our servers.

6
Analyzing and Tracking Your Visitors

In *Chapter 1*, *Preparing and Configuring Your Magento Website*, we looked at how to set up **Google Analytics (GA)** within Magento—particularly how to enable e-commerce tracking.

In this chapter, we will not only be looking at how to interpret the data that we receive, but more importantly how to use it to better optimize our Magento website and continuously improve our conversions.

In this chapter, we will do the following:

- Look at the differences between the many sections specific to e-commerce tracking within GA

- Understand how **Multi-Channel Funnels (MCF)** can help determine the origin of our online sales

- Understand how to track custom events and compare them in relation to e-commerce conversions

- Look at how Universal Analytics will help more accurately describe our e-commerce conversions

- Briefly look at some of the most common A/B testing (content experiment) tools

An overview of e-commerce analytics reports

Once e-commerce tracking has been enabled on our GA profile (as shown in *Chapter 1, Preparing and Configuring Your Magento Website*), we will find many new options available to us across the various sections within GA.

Across most of the pages inside Google Analytics, we can click on the **E-commerce** button within the **Explorer** menu (as shown in the following screenshot) to change the table of data that is presented with data relevant to sales:

By selecting this button on our GA pages, we will be presented with e-commerce-specific data for our chosen section. For example, by navigating to **Behavior | Site Content | Landing Pages** and clicking on the **E-commerce** tab, we will be presented with:

- **Revenue**: Total revenue accrued through customers landing on this page
- **Transactions**: Total number of transactions from this landing page
- **Average Order Value**: How much on average a customer spends after landing on this page
- **E-commerce Conversion Rate**: Percentage rate of visits to sales
- **Per Visit Value**: An average value-per-visit of this landing page

All of this data can be used to better optimize our individual pages and tweak them for improved conversion rates. The same can be said for the e-commerce data provided through the **Explorer** button across many of the GA sections.

One particularly important section that becomes available for us after enabling e-commerce tracking is **Conversions | E-commerce** and everything beneath it, which is shown in the following screenshot:

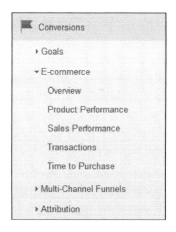

This whole section is dedicated to providing us with e-commerce reports from our Magento store. The following is a brief summary of each of these pages and what we should take from them in order to better analyze our conversion rates:

- **Overview**: This page provides us with a timeline graph of our primary metrics (conversion rate, average order value, quantity purchased, number of transactions, revenue, and so on) so that we can see our sales performance over a specified time period.

- **Product Performance**: This page is useful in evaluating how often each product is ordered and the revenue each individual product is generating.

- **Sales Performance**: This page will, by default, show us the most profitable dates within a given time frame. This is useful to quickly determine whether a specific marketing campaign had a major impact on sales compared to the other dates.

- **Transactions**: This section provides us with the information for each order. Each row contains information such as the specific products purchased (by clicking on **Transactions**), revenue made, tax applied, delivery charges charged, and also the quantity ordered.

- **Time to Purchase**: This page shows either the average days taken from the time a customer first enters our shop to the time they checkout, or (depending on the distribution setting) the number of visits it had taken the customer to eventually purchase.

Adding secondary dimensions and advanced filters

Google Analytics provides us with quick and easy methods for extending the default dataset on these pages and are vital in transforming what are essentially sales reports into sales analytics.

Choosing a secondary dimension allows us to add a column to our default dataset so that we can analyze an entirely different metric alongside our primary dimension.

For instance, this might be useful if we wanted to find out whether our customers were purchasing our products after landing on our home page or whether they were actually landing on our specific product page.

To do this, we would perform the following steps:

1. Navigate to **Conversions | E-commerce | Product Performance** and select **Landing Page** from our **Secondary dimension** drop-down list.

2. We can then see our new column appear next to our product name as shown in the following screenshot:

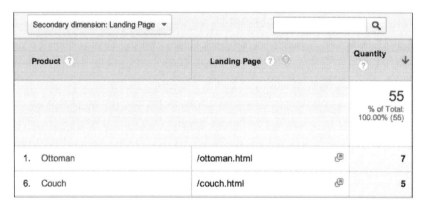

We could then narrow down these results further by using **advanced filters**, for instance, if we wished to narrow our product performance dataset down to a particular brand (where the brand is shown within the product name). To do this, we would perform the following steps:

1. Click on **advanced**, which is located near the search bar to the right-hand side of our **Secondary dimension** setting.

2. Select **Include** from the first drop-down list, **Product** from the second, and **Containing** from the third. We would then enter our brand name into the text box provided.

3. Once we click on **Apply**, our results will be filtered to include only those results where the product name contains our brand.

Advanced segments

As well as secondary dimensions and advanced filters, we should also look at utilizing advanced segments. Google Analytics comes with built-in options for isolating subsets of our traffic.

For example, if we wished to always show data from mobile traffic, we would add **Mobile Traffic** to our advanced segments and then click on **Apply** as shown in the following screenshot:

This will provide us with another row of results specific to **Mobile Traffic** underneath **All Visits** within our dataset.

Custom segments stay active no matter where we navigate through GA, so make sure to return to all traffic in order to view our standard datasets.

For a great tutorial on what we can do with advanced segments, please see (kissmetrics.com) goo.gl/fJzIlM.

Understanding Multi-Channel Funnels

When a customer purchased a product from our Magento website, we used to only be able to see his/her last interaction; that is, the last traffic source that brought the user to our store. With Multi-Channel Funnels, we can now analyze data that has been stored against a customer on the leadup to his/her purchase. Essentially, we are analyzing his/her conversion path.

The standard channel groups that are analyzed are organic search, referrals from other websites, and direct visits.

If we integrate AdWords tracking, we may also see paid search results as a channel along with more advanced AdWords secondary dimensions.

The two main areas within Multi-Channel Funnels for us to have a look at are assisted conversions and top conversion paths.

Assisted conversions

Navigating to **Conversions | Multi-Channel Funnels | Assisted Conversions**, we can see which of our **Channel Groupings** assisted in converting our visitor into a customer. We can also change our dataset so that we can see which of our keywords have assisted our conversions by performing the following actions:

1. Select **Keyword** as our **Secondary dimension** tab.
2. Use the **advanced** filter to only "Include MCF Channel Grouping Containing Organic".

This would be a good technique to find out whether our optimized keywords are making us a return on our SEO campaign.

Top conversion paths

This report shows the number and value of conversions for each unique conversion path. In order to understand this section more clearly, we should add **Keyword (Or Source/Medium) Path** as a secondary dimension. We will then start to see patterns emerge that may help us to understand which channels interact with each other.

For instance, customers who found our website via an organic search might (at a later date) simply enter our website URL into their browser. We can also use advanced filters to filter our **MCF Channel Grouping Path** column to those only containing **Social Network**. We can then, for example, make a more informed decision on whether or not our `Pinterest.com` campaign was worth the investment, as shown in the following screenshot:

For some other quick tips and techniques for Multi-Channel Funnels and using filters, please see (seocandy.co.uk) goo.gl/8xGHlY.

Adding events to track phone number clicks

Event tracking is an extremely useful tool and allows us to track customer interaction with any part of a page. It uses simple JavaScript events, such as `onclick`, to push data to GA so that we can analyze factors that may not be picked up as standard.

A common usage of click-based event tracking would be to analyze how many customers click on our company phone number—possibly in order to get help when browsing our website. Using our e-commerce tracking data, we could then see how many of these events resulted in sales, perhaps giving an indication as to the level of support provided by our telephone operators.

In order to do this, we would simply add the following code to our phone number within the Magento template files (typically within the `header.phtml` file):

```
<a href="tel:555123123" onclick="_gaq.push(['_trackEvent','
   Click-to-Call','Head Area','555-123-123']);">555-123-123</a>
```

In this example, we will track the click event on our phone number and set the following:

- `Click-to-Call` as our category
- `Head Area` as our action
- `555-123-123` as our label

To see the results in GA, we would perform the following steps:

1. Navigate to **Behavior | Events | Overview** and then click on our **Click-to-Call** event category.

 Within primary dimensions, we can also swap between the **Event Action** and **Event Label** options to see a breakdown of our different phone numbers and areas if we are running multiple event-tracking codes.

2. In order to see our e-commerce conversion rates from customers clicking on our phone number, we can click on our **E-commerce** button within the **Explorer** menu to change our table data as shown in the following screenshot:

Event Category	Visits	Revenue	Transactions	Average Order Value
	95 % of Total: 0.32% (29,929)	£5,770.44 % of Total: 5.76% (£100,161.44)	6 % of Total: 0.87% (688)	£961.74 Site Avg: £145.58 (560.61%)
1. Click-to-Call	95	£5,770.44	6	£961.74

We could then use custom segments to further analyze our data; for example, we could display how many of these events were fired from mobile users (as clicking on a phone number is most commonly associated with tablet/mobile devices).

For a fantastic in-depth guide on event tracking, please see this post by *Anna Lewis* (koozai.com) goo.gl/yg0UKu.

Universal Analytics changes the way in which events are triggered using the following code instead:

```
<a href="tel:555123123" onclick="ga('send', 'event',
    'Click-to-Call','Head Area','555-123-123');">
    555-123-123</a>
```

Universal Analytics

The most notable aspect of Universal Analytics in relation to tracking visitors on our Magento store is multiplatform tracking.

For example, the user could perhaps browse our website on his/her mobile phone via a referral link on his/her way to work. When he/she returns home having already learned about our website, he/she could then enter a branded search on Google and purchase our products via his/her laptop.

With standard GA, this would provide us with two visits—one successful conversion through a branded organic search and the other a non-successful referral visit. However, the real-world scenario would be that the "credit" of the sale should be given to the referral visit.

Universal Analytics hopes to resolve this problem by improving its measurement of users accessing the same website across multiple devices.

 Currently (as of Magento CE 1.8), Universal Analytics compatibility is not provided as default within the administration panel; however, there are extensions available that will be covered in *Chapter 8, Purpose-built Magento Extensions for SEO/CRO*.

Implementing and analyzing content experiments

Running content experiments (also known as A/B testing or split testing) is such a far-reaching subject that it could easily be a book in its own right.

As we're trying to cover all the main aspects of Magento SEO, I can only touch upon a couple of useful content-optimization tools that are available and that may help us to increase conversions through adapting the content to better serve our customers.

Google Content Experiments (announced in 2012: goo.gl/yuPcta) allows you to run small snippets of JavaScript on your pages to enable you to track different variations of a page through Google Analytics. Using goals within GA, you can then track the version of the page that is producing the best conversion rate.

An alternative **conversion rate optimization (CRO)** tool that is becoming increasingly popular is Optimizely (www.optimizely.com). Optimizely also uses small snippets of JavaScript, but instead of supplying different pages to different visitors, Optimizely allows you to affect elements on the same page and serve different variations to different visitors. Because of the same URL, it is unfortunately rather difficult to discern any analytical data through GA; therefore, Optimizely supply their own analytics package in order to measure performance data and provide you with the ability to define your own goals.

Both of these tools allow you to adapt the content of your webpage and track the performance of each variation in order to better optimize the user experience. The benefit of Google Content Experiments is that it's integrated into Google Analytics, and as such, we can easily compare our variations to the revenue we have accumulated.

 For a great tutorial on setting up content experiments, please visit (online-behavior.com) goo.gl/51nWWj.

Summary

In this chapter, we have looked at how e-commerce tracking enables a whole host of new features within the Google Analytics panels. We've also seen ways to use secondary dimensions and advanced filters to provide us with more comprehensive reports.

With the implementation of custom event tracking, we've also seen how we can capture the identity of anyone who clicks on the phone number of our website and then goes on to become a paying customer.

We've also looked at how Multi-Channel Funnels provide insights into ways in which different conversion paths interact with one another and how we can better analyze cross-channel marketing campaigns.

A/B testing is a large subject, and we have briefly touched upon the two most popular tools available.

In the next chapter, we will be looking at how we can block search engine access to some of our pages as well as at ways to implement a few tweaks to our `.htaccess` file in order to serve consistent URLs to users.

7
Technical Rewrites for Search Engines

In previous chapters, we have looked at some of the standard adjustments we can make to our `.htaccess` and `robots.txt` files in order to either speed up our website or completely block search engine access to our development site.

In this section, we'll be looking at a few crucial adjustments that we can make to these files in order to further enhance our protection over duplicate-content-related penalties and to reduce the number of unnecessary pages being cached by search engines.

The `.htaccess` and `robots.txt` files that we are editing in this section exist on the root directory of our Magento website.

In this chapter, we will be learning how to:

- Use advanced techniques in the `.htaccess` file to maintain URL consistency and redirect old URLs to their newer equivalents
- Improve our `robots.txt` file to disallow areas that should not be visible by search engines
- Use an observer to block duplicate content issues on filtered category pages

Additional .htaccess modifications

Apart from the in-built URL rewrite system in Magento, we can use the `.htaccess` file to perform complex rewrites on any URL that's requested through our website.

A key part of performing well in search engines is to provide consistent URLs. When we alter our categories/products/pages or even when we migrate from an older website to the Magento format, we must try to redirect users to the new URL path using 301 redirects.

A few common problems that we can resolve through modifying our `.htaccess` file are:

- **Domain consistency**: Ensuring that our domain is always displayed with or without the www prefix (depending on preference)

- Forcing the removal of `index.php` and `/home` from our URLs

- 301 redirecting old pages to their newer equivalents—both static pages and ones that once contained query strings

Maintaining a www or non-www domain prefix

It is important to choose whether we wish to publically display our domain name with or without the www prefix. Websites such as `twitter.com` choose to remove it, whereas many other websites always display it.

Although there are no SEO-related benefits to using either one or the other, it is important that we are not allowing both versions of our website to be accessible simultaneously as search engines see both versions as two completely separate instances of a page.

The easiest way to resolve this is through the Magento administration panel by:

1. Navigating to **System | Configuration | Web**, and then within **Url Options**, we change **Auto-redirect to Base URL** to **Yes (301 Moved Permanently)** as shown in the following screenshot:

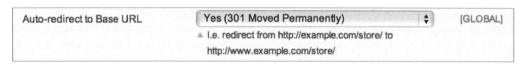

The same result, however, can be accomplished through the `.htaccess` file, and we should implement it also, especially if we are running Magento CE 1.3 or our website contains other publically-accessible pages that are not part of the Magento platform.

To force the www prefix to our domain name, we would first of all set our base URL in system configuration and then add the following code to our `.htaccess` file (replacing `mymagento.com` with our own domain name):

```
<IfModule mod_rewrite.c>
  Options +FollowSymLinks
  RewriteEngine on
  RewriteCond %{HTTP_HOST} !^www.mymagento.com$ [NC]
  RewriteRule ^(.*)$ http://www.mymagento.com/$1 [R=301,L]
</IfModule>
```

To remove www from the URL, we must first of all change our base URLs in the system configuration so that they do not contain www and then replace the preceding code with:

```
<IfModule mod_rewrite.c>
  Options +FollowSymLinks
  RewriteEngine on
  RewriteCond %{HTTP_HOST} !^mymagento.com$ [NC]
  RewriteRule ^(.*)$ http://mymagento.com/$1 [R=301,L]
</IfModule>
```

In the preceding example code, we are essentially asking the server that if the website URL is not exactly mymagento.com (RewriteCond %{HTTP_HOST} !^mymagento.com$ [NC]), we will rewrite everything (.*) to after our non-www domain name, therefore forcing away the www prefix.

Essentially, RewriteCond is used to test our value (in this case our website URL). RewriteRule then performs the redirect but only if those tests (conditions) are passed.

Removing the /index.php/ path once and for all

Within *Chapter 1, Preparing and Configuring Your Magento Website*, we looked at enabling **Use Web Server Rewrites**; however, we will notice that by default, this simply removes the /index.php/ path from our displayed URLs; it doesn't stop them from being accessible using the old path (for example, http://www.mymagento.com/index.php/furniture.html). Apart from this, we will also be able to access our homepage using www.mydomain.com/index.php.

In order to resolve this, we can use a few simple lines of code within our .htaccess file (with or without www):

```
# Removing /index.php/ from any other URL when not in admin
 RewriteCond %{THE_REQUEST} ^.*/index.php
 RewriteCond %{THE_REQUEST} !^.*/index.php/admin
 RewriteRule ^index.php/(.*)$ http://www.mymagento.com/$1 [R=301,L]

# Removing our duplicate homepage
RewriteCond %{THE_REQUEST} ^.*/index.php
RewriteRule ^(.*)index.php$ http://www.mymagento.com/$1 [R=301,L]
```

We may notice that the Magento Connect downloader ceases to operate when we add the preceding code. It is therefore recommended to comment out these lines using # whenever we wish to use Magento Connect (and then uncomment them once completed).

Also, it is important to change the admin path to the correct admin path for your store within the line `RewriteCond %{THE_REQUEST} ^!/ admin/index.php`. Without this line, the Magento admin may not save data correctly.

Redirecting /home to our domain

Apart from being accessible though `www.mydomain.com/index.php`, the home page is also available by default through `www.mydomain.com/home`. This is due to the fact that Magento uses a CMS page as the home page (the `/home` portion of the URL may change depending on the CMS page used).

In order to rewrite `/home`, we can simply perform a standard 301 redirect in our `.htaccess` file (where `www.mymagento.com` is your domain name):

```
redirect 301 /home http://www.mymagento.com
```

Redirecting older pages

Similar to redirecting the `/home` page, we can also redirect any other page to another URL. This is useful if we have an existing website where our old URLs have now been changed.

The two most common types of redirect that we need to apply in these instances are redirect 301 commands and rewrite conditions (for URL parameters).

In order to set up a standard 301 redirect from an old page to the new page, we would simply add the following to the end of our `.htaccess` file:

```
redirect 301 /my-old-page.html http://www.mymagento.com/
  my-new-page.html
```

When we wish to redirect a URL that used to contain a parameter (something that used to be quite common in older e-commerce systems), we need to perform a different type of redirect.

In the following example, we will be redirecting a query string with a specific request to our new product page. This would work for a URL such as `http://www.mymagento.com/my-old-product-page.php?product_id=35`.

```
RewriteCond %{QUERY_STRING} ^product_id=35$ [NC]
RewriteRule .* http://www.mymagento.com/my-new-product.html?
  [R=301,L]
```

 Please note that editing the .htaccess file is always risky; improper configuration will lead to a server error. It is always recommended that the .htaccess file modifications be implemented first on a test environment.

For a fantastic run down on extra modifications including robot-specific blocking, please see the following .htaccess boilerplate (github.com) goo.gl/Gn5i35.

Improving our robots.txt file

As mentioned in previous chapters, the robots.txt file should only be used to let search engines know which pages/paths on the website we wish or do not wish to be crawled. Ideally, we would only want our main pages to be crawled and cached by search engines (products, categories, and CMS pages).

The robots.txt file should be updated whenever a page is created that we do not wish to be crawled; however, the following list is a good place to start and will help to reduce the number of unnecessary pages cached by search engines.

Inside the robots.txt file, we would add the following options (one per line, under User-Agent: *):

Disallow: /checkout/
To stop our checkout pages being crawled

Disallow: /review/
To disallow our product review pages (especially if we are also showing reviews directly on our product pages)

Disallow: /catalogsearch/
To disallow our search-results pages from being indexed by search engines

Disallow: /catalog/product/view/
A further duplicate page where we can view our products by passing the ID

Disallow: /catalog/category/view/

Similar to the preceding option but for categories

> For a further list of possible Magento pages to disallow within the `robots.txt` file, please see the following link (`github.com`) `goo.gl/utyJi0`.

Resolving layered-navigation duplicate content

One of the most common duplicate-content-related issues in Magento comes in the form of layered-navigation-enabled category pages. When we set our categories to be "anchored" (see *Chapter 2, Product and Category Page Optimization*), we allow them to be filtered by certain product attributes.

Magento uses parameters within the URL in order to filter the product collection. The drawback of this is that sometimes these parameters can be cached as separate pages—leading to thousands upon thousands of duplicated category pages.

In an ideal world, the canonical element would take care of this problem, but sometimes our duplicate pages may still be cached by search engines (especially if the website has been live prior to turning on the canonical elements).

One of the most effective solutions to this problem is to use a bespoke function within Magento called an `Observer` function that will perform the following tasks:

- Check to see whether we are viewing a category page
- Check to see whether filters have been activated
- Dynamically modify our `<meta name="robots">` tag to `NOINDEX,FOLLOW`

In order to do this, we need to create a very simple module consisting of a `config.xml` file, an `Observer.php` file, and a module declaration file.

Due to content limitations within this book, we cannot go into detail about how to create a Magento extension from scratch, so instead we'll assume that a module has already been created and that we are free to edit our `config.xml` and `Observer.php` model files.

> For a quick tutorial on setting up Magento extensions, please visit the following link (`magento.com`) `goo.gl/uqDsz3`.
>
> Also, please note that the following functionality is also available for free within the Creare SEO extension mentioned within *Chapter 8, Purpose-built Magento Extensions for SEO/CRO*.

Assuming that our app/code/[codePool]/[namespace]/[module]/etc/config. xml file has been created and set up, we need to add the following code (substituting [module] for our own module name):

```
<frontend>
  <events>
    <controller_action_layout_generate_xml_before>
      <observers>
        <[module]>
          <type>singleton</type>
          <class>[module]/observer</class><!-- replace with
            your module name -->
          <method>changeRobots</method>
        </[module]>
      </observers>
    </controller_action_layout_generate_xml_before>
  </events>
</frontend>
```

The preceding code will register an observer to listen for the controller_action_ layout_generate_xml_before event on the customer-facing side of our Magento installation. This will allow us to adapt the layout XML that has been compiled for our pages and insert our own XML dynamically.

To do this, we need to create our own method that we have mentioned in our config.xml file, changeRobots, which exists inside our observer class located in the app/code/[codePool]/[namespace]/[module]/Model/Observer.php file.

Inside our Observer.php file, we will add the following method:

```
public function changeRobots($observer)
{
  if($observer->getEvent()->getAction()->getFullActionName() ==
    'catalog_category_view')
  {
    $uri = $observer->getEvent()->getAction()->getRequest()-
      >getRequestUri();
      if(stristr($uri,"?")): // looking for a ?
        $layout       = $observer->getEvent()->getLayout();
        $layout->getUpdate()->addUpdate('<reference name="head">
          <action method="setRobots"><value>NOINDEX,FOLLOW</value>
          </action></reference>');
        $layout->generateXml();
      endif;
  }
  return $this;
}
```

In the preceding code, we are checking that our current page is using the action name `catalog_controller_view`; that is, we are viewing a category page. We are then checking for a question mark within the URL request (checking that filters have been activated). If a `?` exists, we add our own XML to our `<head>` block setting the robots' meta tag with the value of `NOINDEX, FOLLOW`.

With this simple implementation, we will add the `NOINDEX` directive to our parameter-based category URLs, essentially asking search engines to remove these URLs from their own indexes.

 For more information on the impact of category filters and duplicate content issues, please visit the following link (`creare.co.uk`) `goo.gl/PfkPAQ`.

Summary

In this section, we have looked at several ways in which we can keep the URLs on our website consistent, especially the home page. Using the `.htaccess` file, we can also redirect old URLs to their new counterparts.

We've also looked at how we can use the `robots.txt` file to disallow unnecessary pages from search engines in order to avoid any duplicate-content-related issues.

We've also seen how category pages can sometimes be duplicated due to active layered-navigation filters and how we can resolve this by using a bespoke `Observer` function to dynamically change our meta information.

In the next chapter, we will be looking at some of the best Magento extensions available that are specifically designed with search engine optimization or conversion rate optimization in mind.

8
Purpose-built Magento Extensions for SEO/CRO

In this chapter, we'll be looking at a selection of SEO and **CRO (conversion rate optimization)** related extensions that should help to bring more visitors to our Magento website and improve our chances of converting those visitors into paying customers.

The decision to make Magento open source is perhaps the primary reason for its meteoric growth over the last few years. The sheer quantity of Magento extensions available through Magento Connect (currently well over 5000) is a testament to the innovate nature of its fantastic community of developers.

Entire companies have been established in order to cater to the demand from the more than 150,000 live Magento stores (according to BuiltWith usage statistics, `goo.gl/H5BbLY`).

In this chapter, we will be looking at:

- Some of the best SEO-specific extensions available for Magento
- CRO-related extensions to help boost sales
- Extensions that enable the use of optional functionality described in this book, such as Universal Analytics and Varnish Cache

Installing extensions

Before we start taking a look at some of the best SEO extensions available for Magento, we should quickly cover their installation.

Most free Magento extensions will be available to install through Magento Connect (`http://www.magentocommerce.com/magento-connect/`).

Paid extensions usually require manual installation; it is therefore important that whoever is installing the extension is familiar with FTP. Most of these types of extensions come with their own set of instructions, and thanks to the automatic setup scripts within Magento, there are never any complicated database adjustments to make.

Generally speaking, the most common problems with extensions can be avoided by making sure that we do this:

- Check that the extension is compatible with our Magento platform (Community/Enterprise/Go)

- Check that the extension is compatible with our own Magento version (for example, CE 1.7)

- Disable Magento compilation prior to installing our extension

- Make sure that our folders are writable by the server

- Check reviews/FAQs for our extension to resolve known issues

- Clear our cache (**System | Cache Management | Flush Magento Cache**) and log out/back in to our Magento admin panel to reset permissions after installing our extension

 For a comprehensive guide on how to install Magento extensions, please visit (`fooman.co.nz` – PDF) `goo.gl/oxnsVl`.

Popular SEO-specific Magento extensions

The following are a selection of the popular extensions related specifically to search engine optimization. The prices and links herein are accurate as of the time of this writing, but may change over time.

SEO Suite Ultimate by MageWorx

One of the most popular full-service SEO extensions out there, SEO Suite Ultimate by MageWorx is reminiscent of the Yoast SEO plugin for WordPress (`goo.gl/oeR500`) in that it supports a wide range of optimization tools within a single extension. Its properties are as follows:

- Type: Paid
- Cost: $399
- Supported for both Community and Enterprise editions

Within its list of features, we will notice several solutions to some of the topics covered in this book (such as rich snippet support/301 redirects for duplicate home pages), and there are also a few unique additions that are worth mentioning:

- The ability to define templates for meta title/description/keywords across all products and categories
- Addition of a simple HTML sitemap for usability
- Ability to edit/choose the canonical URL to use for pages
- XML sitemap improvements including the splitting of the sitemap into several smaller files (great for large Magento sites)
- Ability to define a template for product descriptions (a real time saver!)

Currently, SEO Suite Ultimate will set us back just under $400, which seems a pretty small price to pay for such bold claims by MageWorx as:

> *"It considerably reduces the time necessary for search engine optimization and promotion from 3-6 months to 1-3 months."*

However, I would personally guess that this statement is also dependent on many other ranking factors.

 For more detailed information and to find out about pricing options for multiple installations, we should head over to `goo.gl/mlHbC1`.

Google Shopping feed by Rocket Web

Google Shopping is not a subject that I have touched upon within this book simply due to the fact that the default Google Shopping API within Magento struggles to keep up with the ever-changing Google Shopping requirements.

Thankfully, there is an extension available that seamlessly integrates any type of product into Google Merchant Center. It has the following properties:

- Type: Paid
- Cost: $149
- Supported for both Community and Enterprise editions

A few key features worth mentioning are:

- 100 percent configurable through the Magento administration panel
- Video tutorials available (`goo.gl/iLqenk`)

Google Shopping feeds are becoming CPC-driven and are tied to an AdWords account. To find out more about **Product Listing Ads** (**PLAs**), please see (google.com) goo.gl/NJlLVo.

 For a detailed description and links on where to purchase the Google Shopping feed extension, please visit goo.gl/nNf0yu.

Universal Analytics by Aromicon

Mentioned in *Chapter 6, Analyzing and Tracking Your Visitors*, Universal Analytics is the new tracking method that has been incorporated into Google Analytics.

By default, Magento (<1.8.0.0) does not come equipped with the ability to add our universal tracking code, and so Aromicon have filled that gap in the market with a free extension with the following properties:

- Type: Free
- Supports both Community and Enterprise (although only Community shown on Magento Connect)

Key features:

- Quick and easy installation
- E-commerce tracking enabled

 I would personally recommend disabling the standard Google tracking code within Magento if you are using this extension (**System | Configuration | Google API**).

In rare cases, having both tracking codes may result in duplicate statistics within Google Analytics.

This extension simply swaps out our standard tracking code for the new template using layout XML and custom code in the template, and is therefore really lightweight.

 To download and try out this extension ourselves, we should visit its page on Magento Connect at goo.gl/25Ycwb.

Magento WordPress Integration by FishPig

A regularly updated blog is one of the most common examples of creating fresh content on a website. WordPress is by far the most popular blogging platform on the Internet and can easily be integrated into Magento through the use of this free extension. Its properties are as follows:

- Type: Free
- Supports both Community and Enterprise platforms

The following are a few key features of the Magento WordPress Integration extension:

- Easy access to WordPress features directly though the Magento administration panel
- WordPress categories and posts automatically implement the current Magento theme (no need to retheme the WordPress installation)
- Ability to associate posts with products and categories (similar to related product functionality)

This extension has been downloaded over 50,000 times and just goes to show how popular the combination of using Magento coupled with WordPress has become.

Additionally, there are paid add-ons that can be purchased from `www.fishpig.co.uk` to further extend their already extensive add-on.

 For more information and to download Magento WordPress Integration via Magento Connect, please visit `goo.gl/FJICGr`.

AddThis by AddThis

In *Chapter 2, Product and Category Page Optimization*, we talked about implementing social sharing into our product pages to better "spread the word" about our products through various social media channels.

A really quick and simple extension has been developed by AddThis for us to automatically enable these social widgets on our product pages. Its properties are as follows:

- Type: Free
- Supports both Community and Enterprise

A few key features about this extension are as follows:

- Over 350 different social services supported
- Ability to change social button display
- Smart Layers integration (show follow buttons and recommended content)

Typically, we would only want to display the top four or five social media services (Facebook, Twitter, Google+, and Pinterest).

Alternatively, we could integrate the AddThis widget ourselves if we wanted to place the social icons in custom locations just by visiting their website (www.addthis.com) and downloading their JavaScript snippet.

 For more information on how to get the Magento extension, we should visit the Magento Connect page (goo.gl/iVnKCd).

Creare SEO by CreareGroup

Our final SEO-related extension is a free extension that hopes to solve many of the inherent Magento SEO flaws mentioned within this book. Creare SEO has the following properties:

- Type: Free
- Initially supporting Community Edition

This has been developed by myself and two other Magento Certified Developers at our company Creare Communications Ltd. based in the UK. The Creare SEO extension will feature a large list of functionality including the following key features:

- Dynamic HTML sitemap
- Category H1 headings (as mentioned in *Chapter 2, Product and Category Page Optimization*)
- **Clean-up script**: To empty log tables and generally clean up redundant files
- Layered navigation NOINDEX option for category filters (as mentioned in *Chapter 7, Technical Rewrites for Search Engines*)
- **Default SEO checklist**: To check for default Magento SEO options that have been incorrectly configured

As with SEO Suite Ultimate by MageWorx, our primary goal is to provide the community with a comprehensive yet easily configurable SEO extension that will help to fix most of the SEO-related problems that unfortunately reside within a default Magento installation.

> For a complete breakdown of the functionality (including meta description templates, twitter card support, duplicate product information warnings, and much more) please head over to our page at Magento Connect at goo.gl/chdBRU.
>
> We'd also love to hear your feedback at www.creare.co.uk.

Extensions to help improve CRO

In this section, we'll look at a couple of extensions that will help to improve our conversion rates through user experience. Once again, prices on these pages are accurate as of the time of this publication.

Turpentine by Nexcess

The Turpentine extension allows for Magento to easily integrate into Varnish Cache and also allows Varnish to be configured via the administration panel in Magento.

As mentioned in *Chapter 5, Speeding Up Your Magento Website*, Varnish Cache is a powerful tool that can improve the loading speed of any website. Load speed is increasingly important as more and more Internet-savvy users grow tired of waiting for pages to load.

A faster Magento website will almost certainly result in a higher number of sales. The properties of the Turpentine extension are as follows:

- Type: Free
- Supported for both Community Edition (1.6+) and Enterprise Edition (1.15+)

Some of the key features of Turpentine are:

- Ability to clear cache upon saving of a product/page/category
- Configurable options within the Magento administration panel
- Support for Magento installations within subdirectories

> For more information and to download the extension from Magento Connect, we should visit goo.gl/u0zd0A.

One Step Checkout by OneStepCheckout.com

Checkout optimization, discussed in *Chapter 4, Template/Design Adjustments for SEO and CRO*, is an important factor to consider for any e-commerce website. The simpler the checkout experience, the more likely a customer will enter their details and pay for their product without abandoning their cart.

The default One Page Checkout extension consists of six steps, each step hidden from view until the customer clicks on a button to proceed. This can sometimes lead to shopping cart abandonment as customers are unsure as to how long the checkout process will take.

One Step Checkout simplifies this process by making all required steps visible to the user so that the customer has a good idea of how much information they are required to enter:

- Type: Paid
- Cost: From €245 onwards
- Supported for both Community and Enterprise editions

A few key features of the One Step Checkout extension are:

- It's easy to install because it simply replaces the `/checkout/onepage/` URL with `/onestepcheckout/`
- Admin configuration is used to enable/disable certain fields
- All checkout updates are performed via AJAX, for example, the shipping cost/payment method availability is updated as a customer enters their address details
- It is compatible with most other checkout-related extensions (such as additional payment gateways)

I would personally recommend this extension for any Magento development, and at €245, it is surely worth the price of reducing last-minute shopping cart abandonments.

 One Step Checkout can be purchased directly from the company website (`onestepcheckout.com`).

Noteworthy extension developers

Due to the sheer volume of extensions available, it is impossible to list them all. Instead, here is a list of some of the most recognized Magento extension developers and a selection of their best extensions:

- **Aheadworks** (goo.gl/FSYT9Y): Take a look at Follow Up Email for remarketing and AJAX Cart Pro for CRO and usability

- **Fooman** (goo.gl/JZ3hsb): Take a look at Fooman Speedster for Magento load speed optimization and Fooman Google Analytics+ for enhanced Google Analytics tracking

- **Mage Store** (goo.gl/JxwCJK): Mainly known for their Affiliate+ extension

- **M2E** (goo.gl/KwtIwR): Used for integration into eBay stores and Amazon

- **Amasty** (goo.gl/gX3BUQ): Used for a wide range of usability improvements, such as improved layered navigation

Unlike this book, this list could quite literally never end as more and more companies develop increasingly popular Magento extensions.

Summary

In this chapter, we have looked at how the open source nature of Magento has helped to spawn thousands of Magento extensions through the innovation of its growing community of developers.

We've looked at some of the best SEO-specific Magento extensions available (both free and paid) and have had a quick look at some of the key features of each. We've also looked at a few CRO-related extensions whose aim it is to increase the number of sales we make on our Magento websites.

With the continued expansion of the Magento framework and the ever-increasing demand for third-party solutions, we can expect to see tremendous growth in the Magento Connect marketplace over the coming years.

Index

Thank you for buying
Magento Search Engine Optimization

About Packt Publishing

Packt, pronounced 'packed', published its first book "*Mastering phpMyAdmin for Effective MySQL Management*" in April 2004 and subsequently continued to specialize in publishing highly focused books on specific technologies and solutions.

Our books and publications share the experiences of your fellow IT professionals in adapting and customizing today's systems, applications, and frameworks. Our solution based books give you the knowledge and power to customize the software and technologies you're using to get the job done. Packt books are more specific and less general than the IT books you have seen in the past. Our unique business model allows us to bring you more focused information, giving you more of what you need to know, and less of what you don't.

Packt is a modern, yet unique publishing company, which focuses on producing quality, cutting-edge books for communities of developers, administrators, and newbies alike. For more information, please visit our website: www.packtpub.com.

About Packt Open Source

In 2010, Packt launched two new brands, Packt Open Source and Packt Enterprise, in order to continue its focus on specialization. This book is part of the Packt Open Source brand, home to books published on software built around Open Source licenses, and offering information to anybody from advanced developers to budding web designers. The Open Source brand also runs Packt's Open Source Royalty Scheme, by which Packt gives a royalty to each Open Source project about whose software a book is sold.

Writing for Packt

We welcome all inquiries from people who are interested in authoring. Book proposals should be sent to author@packtpub.com. If your book idea is still at an early stage and you would like to discuss it first before writing a formal book proposal, contact us; one of our commissioning editors will get in touch with you.

We're not just looking for published authors; if you have strong technical skills but no writing experience, our experienced editors can help you develop a writing career, or simply get some additional reward for your expertise.

Magento Responsive Theme Design

ISBN: 978-1-78398-036-9   Paperback: 110 pages

Leverage the power of Magento to successfully develop and deploy a responsive Magento theme

1. Build a mobile-, tablet-, and desktop-friendly e-commerce site

2. Refine your Magento store's product and category pages for mobile

3. Easy-to-follow, step-by-step guide on how to get up and running with Magento

Instant E-Commerce with Magento: Build a Shop [Instant]

ISBN: 978-1-78216-486-9   Paperback: 52 pages

A fast-paced practical guide to building your own shop with Magento

1. Learn something new in an Instant! A short, fast, focused guide delivering immediate results

2. Learn how to install and configure an online shop with Magento

4. Tackle difficult tasks like payment gateways, shipping options, and custom theming

Please check **www.PacktPub.com** for information on our titles

Printed in Great Britain
by Amazon